Bolton Wanderers

First published in Great Britain in 2000 by
The Breedon Books Publishing Company Limited
Breedon House, 3 The Parker Centre, Derby, DE21 4SZ.

ISBN 1 85983 197 4

Printed and bound by Butler & Tanner Ltd., Selwood Printing Works,
Caxton Road, Frome, Somerset.

Colour separations and jacket printing by
GreenShires Group Ltd., Leicester.

Contents

Introduction

THE post-war years were a remarkable era for football as crowds flocked to grounds in numbers never seen before or since. After the austerity of the war years, people wanted entertainment and football was the leisure escape of the masses. And no more was this so than in the industrial towns of Lancashire. Among the clubs that made an indelible mark in this period were Bolton Wanderers, led by Nat Lofthouse, the most illustrious player in their long and proud history.

During the years from the war to their relegation in the 1963-64 season, Bolton Wanderers were among the elite of English First Division clubs. They may have produced teams more workmanlike than elegant, but they were a force to be reckoned with during these glory years. For a club that was one of the Football League's founding members, this is a particularly memorable time.

The highlights were Bolton's participation in two of the most famous FA Cup Finals in history. The first has gone into the records as the 'Matthews Final' when Stanley Matthews inspired a magnificent fightback by Blackpool, who won 4-3 and captured the hearts of all the nation beyond the Bolton town boundaries. In the second, Bolton lifted the Cup, but ensured the vilification of the public at large by beating a post-Munich disaster Manchester United 2-0.

The irony of the Wanderers' two greatest post-war moments coming at times when the world was against them is not lost on Nat Lofthouse himself, who explained, in an interview on Greater Manchester Radio in April 1994: "Bolton was an island surrounded by the opposition. It was unlucky, really, having everybody supporting the other side on the two times we went to Wembley. In the first, everybody wanted Stan Matthews to get his winner's medal. In the second, God forbid, it was after the Munich disaster. If I hadn't been a Bolton player, I would have wanted them to win."

In this industrial town, whose name has been carried throughout the footballing world, thanks to its local club and the international players who have come from its ranks, that they stood alone when all were against them is something the townsfolk are probably quietly proud of. The fortunes of the club may have waned along with the industrial heart of the place, but there is justifiable pride in their history and a deep sense of community. Who knows, the fortunes of both town and team may not be long in enjoying a revival.

Ian Greaves plied his trade as a player at the highest level with Manchester United, appearing on the losing side in the 1958 Cup Final. He also managed Bolton Wanderers after being promoted from the assistant manager's post when Jimmy Armfield moved to Leeds United. After twice coming close to winning promotion, he finally took Wanderers to the top flight in 1978. However, the team struggled and he was sacked in January 1980, with Bolton propping up the division.

He, as much as anyone, is aware of the passions the game excites in the town and the difficulties the club now have in emulating past glories. "You can sense the crowd are thinking 'what are we doing in this league?' They see a modern club, with up-to-date facilities, and they can remember the success of the Fifties and they want it back. Clubs like Bolton Wanderers were among the best when I was playing. For the big matches, the gates are still there for them and for other Lancashire sides that have known better times, like Burnley. Look at how Burnley could get more than 20,000 because the former England star Ian Wright made his debut for them. There is still a hunger for the game in Lancashire."

For Bolton, though, even in their heyday it has not always been good times. There has also been tragedy. The Burnden Park disaster in 1946 was the club's darkest hour when 33 fans died and more than 500 were injured as an estimated 85,000 people crammed into the ground to see an FA Cup tie featuring Stoke City and the legend already that was Stanley Matthews. In 1992, in his role as club president, Lofthouse unveiled a plaque at the ground in memory of those who lost their lives.

On a happier note there is also something about this era that brings back memories of sportsmanship and fair play that appear to have been lost to the modern game. Though make no mistake, there were many hard and uncompromising players about. This is a time that pre-dates satellite television coverage, corporate hospitality and players living the millionaire lifestyles of Hollywood film stars. There was little time, either, for the histrionics indulged in by today's players.

Lofthouse believes there was also a greater empathy between supporters and players. Could it be because the players were earning not much more than the average man in the street, or was it a tacit understanding that the players were doing their best? Perhaps there wasn't the array of television and newspaper punditry waiting to justify their living at every opportunity.

Lofthouse said: "In these days it seems criticism is vital. I think in my day the people who came to watch Bolton Wanderers wanted to see a good game. If that was what they got, then they were quite happy. Of course, they wouldn't have been happy with losing, but at least they thought they had got their money's worth. Nowadays it seems to be that if you keep losing, nobody will support you. The Fifties were a great era in every way."

It sounds too good to be true and Malcolm Barrass is happy to intervene and lift those rose-tinted spectacles just a little, although he has fond memories of his days at Bolton. Like Lofthouse he joined during the war years and like his friend also worked down the pit, while playing as a part-timer on thirty shillings a week. The versatile player who won three England caps at centre-half, but played every position for Wanderers bar outside-right, right-back and goalkeeper, reflects on there not being too much sympathy for the players when the team was losing.

He remembers: "They were great supporters when we were 2-0 up, but at other times they weren't the best in the world to my mind. If you met them in the street after we'd lost a game, their first words would be: 'What were you doing?' They could call you fit to burn, but none of us went out other than to give our best. Nobody goes out to lose."

Barrass was easy enough for the disgruntled fans to track down. There was no need for them to wait outside the players' entrance hoping to catch a brief glimpse before he disappeared in an expensive sports car, though such is the way with today's players. In the early days of his career he caught the bus home and chatted to spectators making the same journey.

The maximum wage meant the players were close to the fans in more than just travel arrangements. Their lifestyles were little better. As the son of Matt Barrass, a professional footballer with Blackpool, Sheffield Wednesday and Manchester City, he had grown up with the life and football was his love. Though he has a confession. Bolton were not his team. He was, and still is, a life-long Manchester City fan. Like many of the players in this era he was financially little better off signing full-time pro forms with Bolton than if he had continued his trade as an engineer and played part-time.

The lack of money in the game may have appealed to the romantics who liked the idea that teams rarely changed. There was little point in moving if the money was going to be the same, and Bolton always enjoyed a good dressing-room atmosphere that encouraged many to stay. With Bolton never being major operators in the transfer market, changes to the first team tended to come about through evolution rather than revolution as long-serving incumbents were replaced by youngsters who had served their apprenticeships in the Reserves and 'A' and 'B' teams.

Yet many of the players knew they were getting a raw deal when at Bolton, average crowds of nearly 30,000 were generating huge revenue. One of those who campaigned vociferously on the issue – and who was eventually to be transferred as a result – was Tommy Banks, one of Bolton's favourite sons and also one of the infamous 'hard men' of the Wanderers side. He was born in Farnworth and played in the local Bolton Boys' Federation during the war. He is famed for his promise to visiting wingers: "Tha'd better not try to get past me unless tha' wants gravel rash." This was a reference to the gravel perimeter track that ran round Burnden Park and where, with a good thumping tackle, wingers were often unceremoniously dumped. However, the reputation tended to detract from the undoubted skills he possessed, which saw him win five England caps in five months in 1958.

Banks made his debut in May 1948, against Wolves, but recalls that when he first signed part-time forms with Bolton Wanderers he was still working down the pit. With his money from football and his pit wages, he was on almost as much as the leading players in the Bolton side. He regards it as an indictment of the pay which players received at the time and the reason why he first refused to sign for Wanderers full-time. He had also received offers from both Wolves and Manchester United, but with the wages the same, there was little to choose between them.

"The manager, Walter Rowley, asked me to come out of the pit and said I would be in the team by the time I was 21," he said. "He also said I would play for England if I gave up mining, but I told him I was all right. Rowley warned my career would go no further if I didn't do as he wanted. I have always been a bit of an opinion man and I speak my mind. The system was all wrong and players had no say. I remember Tom Finney having the chance to go to Italy because Roma were interested, but Preston North End wouldn't let him go and that was it. In the end, speaking out got me the sack because I had too much to say when we were looking for a better deal in the early Sixties."

He argues that while there is little point in comparing the sort of money he earned with the pay packets modern footballers can expect to receive, few realise that during the Fifties wages didn't keep pace with the levels they had been at in the mid-Thirties in relation to the average wage. In the Thirties, a miner's wage was £2 10s while Bolton players were on £8 in winter and £6 in summer. By the Fifties, the footballers' money had risen only to £12 and £8 and many workers were taking home close to that, if not the same. At £2 and £1 respectively, the bonus for a win and a draw was the same in 1957 as it had been in 1923.

Banks acknowledges, though, that football was special at this time because there was nothing else. He recalls that local football was huge. He had started out playing for a local boys' club called Partridges, but every district had its own teams and everybody was taking part and there were a lot of good footballers to look up to and learn from.

While he would have liked his contemporaries to be better rewarded for their talents, he is keen to emphasise they were great times and he has some wonderful memories of this era. And he wonders whether the modern players get to enjoy themselves as much as their predecessors did now they are constantly under the public spotlight. The regular players' after-match outing into Manchester, with wives and girlfriends, for a meal and then on to a club certainly never attracted the media attention it would for Premiership players now doing the same.

Eddie Hopkinson, who was the England and Bolton goalkeeper and played in the 1958 Final, is keen to point out that football provided a good living for the players in the post-war years. "I was on £70 a week at the end of my career in 1969 and when people ask me if I would like to play nowadays and earn £10,000, then of course I would. But when I played it was the game and not the financial reward that was important. We had a good living compared to other people after the war. When I started playing, the war had only been over for five years."

Gordon Taylor, now chief executive of the Professional Footballers' Association, was determined the association should buy a painting, *Going To The Match*, by L. S. Lowry because in his view it is the definitive football picture of a golden age. The picture was painted in 1953 and the crowds depicted are heading towards Burnden Park, with the industrial chimneys in the background. It captures that feeling of excitement and nerve-tinging anticipation before a big game.

After a successful schoolboy career, Taylor attracted the attention of a number of clubs, including Arsenal and Manchester United, but when given the chance to join Wanderers, the club he had supported since his father took him to games from the age of eight, there was no doubt where he would go. To appear alongside players he had queued to see was a dream come true. As he says, he still has the programmes from the matches when he went as a spectator, and years later to have his own name in the programme was a great thrill.

The sportsmen of the day were certainly *Boys' Own* heroes unsullied by tabloid newspaper revelations. Ian Greaves remembers as a schoolboy seeing Stanley Matthews play in a wartime game at Rochdale. When the ball went out of play, the youngster threw it back over the white-washed wall to the legend himself. For weeks to come he recounted the tale to his friends.

Roy Hartle, virtually ever-present in the Bolton side from 1955, having signed professional in 1952, has his own view of why this particular time was an exceptional one. "The thing that made it special was the players you were playing with and the camaraderie we had. Most of us came through the 'A' and 'B' teams, then into the Reserves, before making the first team. You sort of grew up with each other, which always helps. Today, players are brought from all over the world. It can't be the same."

He also believes that one beneficial result of the maximum wage was that there was no jealousy in the dressing-room, centred on what other players were earning. Everybody was on the same. It prevented divisions and ensured everybody helped each other by generating a strong team spirit. There were also no agents waiting in the wings. Hartle believes they have proved a curse in the modern game.

He echoed Barrass when he added: "I always refer back to the days when I used to go down on the bus with the spectators. We came back on the bus with them as well. If we hadn't done particularly well, we were with twenty to thirty people who had been at the game and would let you know it. We were much closer to the fans. Not just travelling on the bus with them, but we would be out shopping in the town with our wives and children, the same as them.

"Now the fans never see the players. They turn up, play, get in their cars and disappear until the next game. We were on £12 a week when the man on the shop floor was probably on £8 or £9. There wasn't the vast difference there is nowadays with players earning thousands a week."

Another change in the modern game he laments is that the art of tackling has gone. Certainly those of a certain age, who have been regular habitués at Burnden Park through the decades, must miss seeing the home full-backs hitting opposing wingers so hard they ended up on the gravel track. Given that with Banks the two were among the most feared full-backs in the game, it is not surprising that Hartle regrets that some of the physical contact has gone. He believes the game is poorer for it. In place of the ferocious tackle has come shirt pulling, obstruction and feigning injury, all traits he deplores.

He also admits that like many of the supporters he can't name the players in many of the sides that visit Bolton's modern Reebok Stadium. "If I recognise two or three, I have done well. In my day the supporters could name eight or nine of the visiting players and when we played away, their fans knew us because we played together that much. I think these days it seems teams in the lower half of the Premiership and the First Division change their line-ups almost for the sake of it. We tended to only change if there was a player injured."

Hartle is now president of the supporters' club and a view frequently expressed at social events is that football is no longer about the man in the street. Sadly, it seems the average supporter is no longer an important part of the game. What matters nowadays is the corporate client paying £2,000 a year. The average fan is being priced out.

For some, though, the cost just has to be borne because, for them, the club can become more than just a Saturday afternoon out. As Tom Hodgkinson, chairman of the Bolton Wanderers Supporters' Club, which he helped found in 1992, explains, it can become a life-long obsession. He was at Burnden for the Stoke City game that ended in tragedy, and on the field he has seen the highs and lows in nearly six decades since. As he says, the Wanderers are in his blood.

As they are for Florence Brandwood, and for Fred and Florence Guest. All are life-long fans and are proof that football encompasses not just all ages, but all classes. Brandwood remembers working in the town's mills where the talk would be of the local football team and its chances the following Saturday. Above the din of the machinery, the workers struggled to make themselves heard or lip read, much in the manner caricatured by the late comedian Les Dawson. It was Brandwood who suggested the club should have a young boy as mascot and her son, David, was the second to be chosen. The picture of him in his kit with the players is deeply cherished.

Brandwood also recounts when she risked the sack to watch an FA Cup midweek replay. Given a choice between Wanderers and her job, it was no contest, although the boss was eventually to rescind his decision as the mill was short of staff. She says: "I couldn't live if I didn't see Bolton Wanderers. What would I do in winter if there was no Wanderers? I love football." This is a dedicated fan who has queued through the night to secure tickets for key Bolton games. Who has expended a considerable part of her disposable income to pursue the team. And who, when taken ill at a FA Cup game, refused to be taken to hospital because she feared she would be kept in and miss the replay four days later.

The Guests also have a lifetime's devotion to the club behind them. They owned a large stationery business in Bolton and were on first-name terms with many of the players. Indeed, Florence Guest remembers they once employed Willie Moir as a sales representative. Moir, a Scottish international, played twelve years at Bolton and captained the side in the 1953 FA Cup Final. He proved a better football forward than a salesman she recalls. The problem was not the fault of the player. He was able to get his foot in the door without any difficulty, but potential customers were not interested in stationery. All they wanted to talk about was football.

Bert Gregory joined the Wanderers staff as a general handyman just after the war and remained until 1981. He has fond memories of his time at Burnden Park, where he was on first-name terms with all the players. "It was a wonderful club to be involved in. By and large they were a great set of men; there were some wonderful blokes. In those days most of them were locals. If not from Bolton itself, then certainly the North West."

Certainly with a team packed with locals, if the football club did well there was a general buzz in the whole community. People set off for work on a Monday morning with a livelier spring in their step. And in this largely working class industrial town there was a recognition that what the Wanderers lacked in playing resources and state-of-the-art facilities they made up for with determination and hard work. The club's motto is "Supera Moras," translated as "Overcome All Difficulties," and during the years after the war, the Wanderers players turned doing just that into an art form.

Yet a cherished thought of Gregory provides a fitting final note for those about to dip into a deep pool of nostalgia. He remembers the teams in those far off days were so constant that "you could recite them like you were reciting poetry". But the players whose names he reels off are not of the Fifties vintage. He pre-dates those teams by a good few years. It is the team of the Twenties, who won three famous FA Cup Final victories in 1923, 1926 and 1929 using only seventeen players, that he recalls.

For it is the way with sport that the teams and players of our youth are the ones that bring back the fondest memories. So for those of a certain age the following chapters will hopefully revive happy times. For others they will begin to give an insight into a golden era. But let us not forget that for today's youngsters, the team that came so close to the first Wembley Final of the new millennium will, in years to come, feature fondly in their own trips down memory lane.

Tragedy at Burnden Park

W ITH the war over, football was beginning to generate huge interest and a good Cup run in the 1945-46 season saw Bolton gripped with excitement as the second leg of a sixth-round tie against Stoke City approached. With a 2-0 lead from the first match, thanks to two Ray Westwood goals, hopes were high that the Wanderers would progress.

As the day of the game approached, what helped whet the appetites of the home fans even more was that with Stoke City being the opponents, the talismanic figure of Stanley Matthews would be playing. The game, though, was to be remembered not for the dribbling wizardry of Matthews, but as one of the darkest chapters in the annals of the game.

In the aftermath of the tragedy that unfolded that day, crowds gathered on street corners in the mill town to take in the news. Mothers, wives and girlfriends waited to welcome home loved ones. For some the wait was in vain. Thirty-three supporters died and their bodies were laid out on the pitch before being taken to temporary morgues. Another 500 were injured. It was to be Bolton Wanderers' blackest hour, and for Matthews his most tragic match.

A huge crowd had been expected, of course. But the numbers surpassed even the most optimistic predictions. The official figure gives an attendance of 65,419, but probably more than 85,000 had been shoehorned into a ground not fully open because part of the Burnden Stand was being used to stockpile food. Many had gatecrashed what they hoped would be a party, only to be witness to a wake. The huge numbers meant the ground was a potential disaster just waiting to happen.

One of those who joined the throng heading for the game was 12-year-old Tom Hodgkinson. Already a committed Wanderers fan, he had followed the team through the early Cup rounds. He hadn't been at the previous Cup games where Blackburn Rovers, Liverpool and Middlesbrough were dispatched, but had followed the news in the local paper and listened to the opinions of the grown-ups. He and his pals now debated the chances of a Cup Final appearance.

On the match day itself, he had caught a tram with a friend from his home in a suburb of Bolton and as it approached Manchester Road and the ground, the crowds were beginning to swell, but that was nothing new. Watching the throng move shoulder to shoulder down the road, with the tramlines in the middle, was something that gave the youngster nothing to fear. Indeed, as he will recount, he was to be oblivious to the danger he faced, even as the tragedy itself unfolded. Yet only good fortune spared his life as he stood on the embankment that day.

Well over fifty years later, his own words give the best testimony to the Burnden Park disaster as witnessed by a young boy. "I remember it was an early kick-off because there was no such thing as floodlights in those days. We knew it was a big game and there was a sense of urgency. But it was more being desperate to get into the ground. The idea that anything bad could happen never crossed our minds. As kids we were also looking forward to seeing Stanley Matthews in action. We knew, though, that we would win.

"There was a big queue, but then again there always was and we took our turn and got into the ground. We made our way to the back of the embankment as we thought we had the chance of a better view. There were always big steps, it was a very deep terrace and we hoped we would be able to see the game.

"At the back of the embankment were walls made out of railway sleepers and we got close to them, about three steps from the back. There was no such thing as segregating the supporters and I remember there were some Stoke City supporters in there and some good-natured banter between our fans and them.

"As the kick-off approached, it was obvious the ground was getting very full, but we weren't worried. All we were concerned about was that, as it got more crowded, there was less chance of us being able to see. We thought about trying to get nearer to the front, but there would have been even less hope of us being able to view the game, so we decided to stay at the back.

"Although I now know that people were beginning to be crushed, at the time we never felt anything was out of the ordinary. Even as the players ran out, we could just about see and were hoping that we would be able to watch the whole game.

"But shortly after the kick-off we could see people climbing over the sleeper walls to try to get in, and we assumed that the gates had been locked because the ground was full. Now it was starting to be a real crush. We were being pressed shoulder-to-shoulder and chest-to-chest. I've no idea how far into the game it was. We couldn't see anything of the match anyway."

Then Hodgkinson remembers a voice in the crowd uttering the words that probably saved the lives of himself and his 14-year-old friend. "We'd better get these children to the front somehow," was the cry. The response was to hoist the two high into the air and pass them over the heads of the crowd. But young Hodgkinson was upset because they were not heading for the front and what, in their eyes, would be a potentially wonderful view of the match.

He recalls: "Instead of us heading towards the playing pitch, either through the pressure of the crowd or the wisdom of the men handling us, we were actually pushed towards the entrance. As far as viewing the match was concerned, it was a worse position than we had been in originally. We couldn't see a thing, but we were still hoping to watch the Cup-tie. Given that I was only about four foot six at the time, with hindsight it was a bit optimistic."

Eventually they were encouraged to leave the ground altogether, and since they could hear the roar of the crowd but could see nothing, it seemed the best thing to do. However, rather than go home they hung about outside. And so as the bodies were recovered from the crush, they joined a group of youngsters who had also failed to see the game and were behind the stand playing their own football match with a tin can as a ball. For an hour or so they dreamed they were scoring vital Cup goals for Wanderers.

When the time to go home arrived, they set off back and walked up Manchester Road with adults who had also been unable to see the game and had given it up as a bad job. It didn't make them feel as bad. Of the tragedy they still knew nothing.

"It was nearly an hour and a half after I left the ground that I finally got home and my mother was waiting for me. 'It's just been on the radio, there's been a lot of trouble at Burnden,' she told me. I went out to play and it was only when I arrived back at the house that I heard people had been killed.

"Not seeing the game had been disappointing, but thankfully I had come out of it in one piece. Throughout the day I'd never felt frightened. It's only now that I realise what a godsend it was that I got pushed to the edge and the entrance rather than down to the front."

There was another outcome of the tragedy. "After that, my mother banned me from going to Wanderers for the rest of the season. And even later, I was only allowed to go if she thought it was a game that wouldn't attract a big crowd."

What the young Hodgkinson could not have realised, as he stood on the terrace that day, was that as the crowds in the embankment swelled and the crush started to generate panic, the police ordered the turnstiles closed, but the head checker couldn't be found. There was now a situation with people trying to leave because a view of the match was impossible, while others impatiently pressed to get in.

Spectators poured on to the perimeter track, first of all in the north-west corner. Even with the turnstiles finally closed, people were still gaining admittance by climbing over the wall or forcing turnstiles. A father who picked the lock on a gate next to the boys' entrance to enable his young son to get out, unwittingly let in a further surge of supporters. The overall pressure was such that two barriers collapsed and fans were crushed.

Fred Guest was also at the match that day, with his elder brother, and as the crowd swelled he sensed something was wrong. He had already been to the 1929 Cup Final to watch Bolton and had seen most of the big matches since, but the pressure of the crowd for this Cup-tie was something he had never experienced before.

He said: "My brother said to me that something bad was going to happen. We climbed on to a big concrete post to get away from the crush and saw people lying on the ground. I didn't realise they were dead at the time. Looking back, it is one of the saddest things I have ever witnessed – and certainly my worst moment watching Wanderers."

He said that the 1989 Hillsborough disaster, when Liverpool fans were crushed during an FA Cup semi-final, was reminiscent of the Bolton tragedy. As at Burnden Park, more and more people crowded in and there was nowhere for them to go. Ninety-six people died in that disaster. During the Burnden tragedy he was able to see the game, but remembers very little of it other than that Matthews seemed to be at his best, cruising down the wing with nobody able to stop him. He also recalls that both he and his brother thought people had been injured, but neither could believe there had been fatalities. Not at a football match.

In the Stoke City dressing-room before the game, the players had been given their final instructions from manager Bob McGrory, who urged them to throw themselves into the game from the off, to try to overturn the deficit. Despite being two goals in arrears from the first leg, there was confidence in the visitors' ranks.

That it was a huge crowd was obvious as they ran out, but it was expected for the Cup-tie. The match at Stoke had seen an attendance of more than 50,000. Supporters spilling out on to the terracing to get a better view was also not unusual. What quickly became apparent, though, was that this crowd was pouring on to the playing surface itself.

In his autobiography *The Stanley Matthews Story,* the great player says: "Then I got the feeling that there was more in this sudden invasion than met the eye." It was only after the game had been halted and the players reached the sanctuary of the dressing-room that the news was relayed that there had been deaths on the terraces.

Bert Gregory had known it would be a big gate and was looking forward to a glorious Cup-tie. He had even asked his wife if she wished to go and his position as general handyman at the club meant he was able to obtain a couple of stand tickets well away from the mayhem. With his knowledge of the ground, though, he knew this was a bigger crowd than anticipated. Even getting into the ground, he witnessed pushing and shoving, but was not affected, having tickets for seats near the front.

He said: "I knew it looked like a big crowd and I wasn't surprised. People had been starved of football during the war and this was a big Cup-tie that everybody had been talking about. We got settled and comfortable in our seats. It was only after the match started and I saw how unusually large the crowd was in the embankment, that I thought there was going to be trouble.

"The fact is, the ground wasn't geared up for big crowds. They couldn't get the stewards, partly because of the war. It meant there was nobody marshalling the crowds and I could see the terrace swaying."

When the match kicked-off, the crowd was still spilling on to the pitch. While Gregory was still not unduly concerned, his wife was starting to get worried and he tried to reassure her. Her premonition was that somebody would be hurt, but he tried to quieten her fears.

Gregory recalls: "You could see the crush and people were spewing on to the field, encroaching on the play. I had seen crowds do that before and was still unaware of just how serious things were. When the referee took the players off, you could see one or two people being carried on to the field.

"I told my wife they had just fainted and we could see the first-aid people with them, but I was now uncomfortable myself. My wife screamed: `Some of them are dead.' I tried to reassure her. Then we saw a women carried on to the pitch and they covered her face with a cloth. I still remember that scene after all these years."

And he adds: "All I kept thinking to myself was that this doesn't happen at a football match. People don't die at a football match. Yet all the while, I watched bodies being carried away, others were walking away with injured arms while there were some on stretchers. Eventually they got everything cleared and the police pushed the crowd back as best as they could."

On the advice of the Chief Constable of Bolton, the game was ordered to be resumed. The police view was that this would prevent any disorder among the crowd. It was a curious aspect of the disaster that the majority of those inside the stadium were unaware of the events unfolding. It would only be later as the sports edition of the local evening paper hit the streets that the extent of the fatalities became widely known.

About hearing the news that the game was to be completed, Matthews wrote: "We got up and sadly walked down the tunnel on to the field once more. One angry spectator, who must have been told about the deaths, caught hold of Frank Baker, the outside-left, and shouted: 'Tis a crime to carry on.' This was silly talk, we were doing our job. As footballers we came under the orders of the referee; and if he said play, then play we did."

To accommodate the numbers, the police had opened the Burnden Stand for 1,000 spectators while others were at the edge of the pitch. A fresh line had been made with sawdust restricting the playing area. The first half ended goalless but as the players went to make their way to the dressing-rooms, the instruction came to play on without the break. The reasoning was that a break would have a depressing effect on the players and with the fans becoming aware of what had happened, continuing play would keep their minds occupied.

Stoke had the best of the second half but could not find the net and Bolton were through to the next round. They would progress no further as they were beaten in the semi-finals by Charlton Athletic at Villa Park, by two goals to nil.

The dressing-rooms at Burnden were not the only ones shrouded in gloom that day as players were told of the tragedy. The reserve team were playing against Newcastle United Reserves and after the match, word was received that there had been a disaster at Burnden.

Malcolm Barrass played in that match and recalls his sense of shock and fear when he heard. He knew his father was going to the game and remembers many of the other players had relatives or friends who were planning to go to what was billed as an exciting Cup-tie.

He said: "We knew nothing of the number of casualties then, but on the journey home, when we stopped for something to eat, we were told there had been deaths. Everybody was numb. It was a terrible shock. Later, I learned from friends who played for a local works team, and who had been on the embankment, that they had been bent down to within a few feet of the floor with the weight of people pressing down."

The town of Bolton was stunned by the disaster and the mayor opened a relief fund which was swelled by charity matches including England versus Scotland at Maine Road. It collected nearly £40,000, a not-inconsiderable sum in the Forties.

There was also an enquiry ordered by the Government of the day, headed by Moelwyn Hughes KC, which lasted five days during March and April. Its findings were that there was no blame that could be attached to anybody for the disaster. The expectation of a 50,000 attendance was considered reasonable. The truth was that the crowd had been unwittingly responsible for its own fate. However, a series of recommendations relating to the reception and control of crowds, not only at Burnden but throughout the Football League, was put forward.

The Home Office report's recommendations for the embankment were carried out at a cost of £5,500. They included the installation of new turnstiles, which was a task that fell to Bert Gregory as club handyman. He had also been extensively questioned by the police following the tragedy.

He explained: "I was shocked by the disaster and couldn't believe it, but it fell to me to deal with the police, who asked me lots of different questions. The club manager, Walter Rowley, sent for me and said that what had happened was a terrible thing but said I was to be careful what I said to the police. I couldn't give them anything anyway. It was one of those things; very sad but nothing could be done about it."

The Early Seasons: 1946 to 1950

A S THE war drew to a close, Bolton again showed the winning touch in Cup competitions that had served them so well in the Twenties and would do so again in the Fifties. They battled their way to the Football League (North) Cup Final which had helped provide competitive football in the war years. The Final was to be against Manchester United and the jinx they so often seemed to hold over their close neighbours was to come into its own again.

Wanderers had already notched two-legged victories against Blackpool, Newcastle and Wolves and their opponents were now a United team which played its home games at Maine Road because Old Trafford was bomb-damaged. The two-legged Final in 1945 was to be watched by more than 100,000 people as football again began to attract huge support.

Rivalry between Bolton Wanderers and Manchester United has always been intense, and continues so to this day. Perhaps United have always been the big city glamour club and Bolton the small town poor relation. Yet during the war years and beyond, it was the Wanderers who often proved to be the bogey side for their more illustrious neighbours from just down the road.

Ian Greaves remembers: "Bolton Wanderers were always a bit of a menace to us at Manchester United. It was always a local derby and usually in their favour. I remember playing at Burnden and it was very foggy and we were convinced it should have been abandoned. We lost 5-2 and I scored an own-goal. Matt Busby dropped me and I asked him how he could possibly have seen how I played, when he couldn't see across the pitch."

Greaves could never understand the cause of the animosity Bolton fans had for Manchester United, but knows it has always been there and is not mutual. "It is a funny relationship between Bolton fans and Manchester United. They hate the club passionately and I have no idea why. It certainly pre-dates the Munich air disaster and the 1958 Cup Final. Perhaps it is that between the two clubs, Bolton have been the underdogs for so long."

Passionate supporter Florence Brandwood can enlighten him. "There are a few clubs which we have always hated. With United it probably got worse after the 1958 Cup Final because everybody was against us. The real reason we have never liked them, though, is they have always been bad losers. It's the same today with Alex Ferguson. We didn't like losing, but we were good losers – and they never were."

She said that after the war there was huge enthusiasm for the game. Rationing was still on, and times were hard, but football was a cheap day out to be looked forward to. She would walk the three miles from her home, or buy a neighbour ten cigarettes in return for a ride on the back of his motorbike.

Brandwood added: "I always used to get to the ground early. You had to because I've known full houses at Burnden after the war. I stood in the same place on the embankment and knew the people all around me. It was a ritual. I remember years later when Stan Mortensen was manager at Blackpool, he recognised me from his playing days as he walked around the ground. 'You're not still here are you?' he asked before he had a quick word with me."

There was also, though, sadness in these times. Football returned, but some of the players from the pre-war days did not. In particular, Brandwood remembers Harry Goslin because, not only was he the captain when war was declared, but her son David would later play club cricket with Goslin's son. Goslin had joined Wanderers in 1930 and made his debut that year against Liverpool. He was appointed skipper six years later. His last appearance for Bolton was at York in March 1942. He was killed the following year in Italy.

When it came to the Football League (North) Cup Final itself, Wanderers struggled in the opening exchanges, despite having Nat Lofthouse back after injury. But then, so too did Manchester United and in a strong wind which mitigated against too many chances being created, the game was scoreless at the break. The decisive goal came in typical Lofthouse fashion; a well-taken corner by Woodward had goalkeeper Jack Crompton in difficulties and both player and ball ended up in the back of the net after the centre-forward's charge.

That settled the first leg in Bolton's favour and the Cup was won a week later after a hard fought 2-2 draw with United at Maine Road. It was the venue for the Manchester club because Old Trafford had been damaged in a wartime air raid. It was a knife-edge finish, though, with Barrass bringing the visitors level in the final minute.

To cap it all, a 2-1 win over Chelsea at Stamford Bridge decided the North v South Final in the Lancashire club's favour. With the war about to end and the resumption of League football close, Bolton were in good footballing health for the future.

Eventually, as though frozen in time, the fixture list from the 1939-40 season was resurrected seven years later and on August 31, 1946, before 62,850 fans at Stamford Bridge, the biggest crowd the Bolton players would perform before all season, it was business as usual for the Football League.

Victory went to the London side, but Wanderers' players and supporters were claiming a moral victory in a game that should have been won, but slipped from them 4-3. Moral wins, though, don't provide valuable League points and although there were claims that a refereeing blunder had gifted the home side a goal against the run of play, Wanderers should have done more with their attacks, but three times the woodwork denied them early on. Two goals for young Nat Lofthouse gave a glimpse of the League form that would serve Bolton well for the next fourteen years.

Predictions that this would be a massive season, as far as numbers turning up to support the game, were confirmed with this match. It proved a financial windfall for Bolton who were on a share of the gate. Less welcome was the crush outside the ground as thousands of spectators tried to get through the turnstiles. Just months after the Burnden Park tragedy, it graphically highlighted that lessons had not been learned and fans were still being poorly served. It would remain the case for more than three decades until the deaths of 96 Liverpool supporters attending a FA Cup semi-final at Hillsborough brought widespread changes to improve ground safety.

The verdict from Malcolm Barrass on the Wanderers' side as the Forties came to a close, can be summed up in one word. It was "workmanlike." He adds: "Some of the lads had only just got back from the war and they were a good bunch. The atmosphere was always good among the players. We were, though, a struggling team and we were relegation candidates more often than not. What kept us up was blood and guts. We had some good players, but we were more of a solid side than anything else and nobody would call our play pretty."

That relegation was more of an issue than any top-of-the-table considerations is highlighted in the statistics: throughout the late Forties, when League football returned, Bolton always finished in the bottom half of the table with a fourteenth place in the 1948-49 season being the best they could manage. For a side with a great tradition in the Cup, the results here were also disappointing. Winning the Lancashire Cup in 1948 against Southport, courtesy of a Willie Moir hat-trick, was not exactly the fans' idea of Cup glory.

If Bolton were able to often overcome the form book in their encounters with Manchester United, then it was the reverse of the coin with Manchester City. The FA Cup dreams of 1933 and 1937 had both been ended by the Maine Road side, and in January 1947 fans arrived hoping for revenge as City were the visitors for a fourth-round encounter. City were in the Second Division, but were about to prove a bogey team again.

Yet all appeared to go well for the home side with a goal in thirty seconds. Lofthouse found Woodward, whose early cross was collected by Wrigglesworth inside the penalty area. His shot left the legendary goalkeeper Frank Swift well beaten. A Lofthouse header nine minutes later meant Bolton were in control. Two second-half goals by Black, though, brought City level and it was the visitors who took the lead when Capel took full advantage of a poor clearance by Stan Hanson. With time running out, Barrass ensured there would at least be a replay. It was a temporary reprieve as four days later, City won 1-0.

Eddie Hopkinson remembers when he arrived at Wanderers, it was a great side because of the characters, although the first team tended to train separately from the rest and also didn't train as hard. Their experiences of having fought in the war had given the older professionals a different outlook on life.

He explained: "We've gone back to a squad system where the whole squad train together, but we didn't really have that then. A lot of these guys had fought in the war. They had come back and a lot of their mates had been killed. Life was to be worth living for them. Playing football, they were getting good money even though it can't be compared to today. They were a little bit wild and lived for today. They had seen so many people alive today and dead tomorrow in six years of war. There were some wonderful people. It was an interesting time."

For many of the Wanderers' pre-war heroes, the break for hostilities had robbed them of their best years and now was the time to make way for new blood. It fell to the manager Walter Rowley to bring the curtain down on the Burnden Park careers of such players as Ray Westwood, Albert Geldard, George Hunt and Harry Hubbick.

Westwood, in particular, had been a loyal servant and star attraction at the club since joining as an amateur in 1928 and turning professional in March 1930. He played more than 300 games for the club and scored 144 goals in League and Cup. His prowess at inside-left brought international honours and he won six caps for England. He was famed for his speed, body-swerve and superb ball control.

Wanderers were strengthening and would soon be packed with internationals and, indeed, boast an all-international forward line. The days of relegation battles would then be a thing of the past as the side that emerged could stand comparison with any produced before or since at Burnden Park.

Football clubs in this era enjoyed large playing staffs, a situation helped by the maximum wage. As Gordon Taylor points out, it meant that Wanderers had full-time professional players not just in the first team and the Reserves, but in the 'A' and 'B' sides as well. With players returning from the war, competition for the first-team shirts was fierce. At full-back, for example, there was a surfeit of riches. Tommy Banks and Roy Hartle now found themselves banished to the Reserves for a few years. Their day would come later.

On September 7, 1946, it was the chance to play in front of the home fans for the first post-war League game at Burnden Park. Five players who had enjoyed victory in the fixture when it marked the last game before the war – Hanson, Hubbick, Howe, Westwood and Rothwell – were back in the white shirts for this encounter. A penalty miss after Lofthouse was brought down in the 27th minute meant the opportunity to open the scoring and settle nerves had been squandered. Tom Hamlett was the culprit, kicking straight at Walker who saved easily.

Portsmouth had their chance when Froggatt hit the post after the break, but there was controversy as the match entered its final minutes. The referee awarded a penalty to the visitors after Stan Hanson in the Bolton goal had brought down Froggatt. However, at the insistence of Bolton players, he consulted a linesman and reversed the decision.

If Pompey players were furious at the referee's action, then their anger was exacerbated seconds later when Willie Moir scored the winning goal for Bolton. The idea that in those far-off days, players accepted the judgment of the officials in good grace was not always the case. In a scene reminiscent of a modern Premiership game, when the referee brought a halt to proceedings three of the Portsmouth players had to be dragged away from the linesman they believe robbed them of a penalty and victory.

A measure of the new passion for football since the war was reflected in the attendance figures. Before the war there had been only 12,992 though the turnstiles for this fixture. This time the sides played before a crowd of 33,597.

The 1948-49 season underlined the view of Barrass that, for most of the seasons just after the war, the ambition for Bolton was to avoid a relegation dogfight rather than offer a serious challenge. By the last game of the season, First Division survival was never in danger, but the patience of the fans was wearing thin as the side managed only three victories from the New Year until the season's close. It included a 5-0 drubbing by Arsenal in the February.

However, more than 22,000 of the Burnden Park faithful saw an upbeat finish to the season with a sterling performance against Everton that deserved more than a one-goal reward. In the 21st minute, Moir connected with a Woodward free-kick near the corner flag to beat Ted Sagar with a header, the force of which brought the ball back into play before many realised it had been in the net. Moir's goal was his 25th of the campaign and ensured he topped the League's goalscoring table for the season.

Only two of the players from the pre-war era now remained – Hanson and Howe – as changes saw the beginnings of a new side. The next decade would see the rise and break-up of two sides. The first would contest the 1953 FA Cup Final. The second would visit the Twin Towers in 1958. Only two players would figure in both: Nat Lofthouse, of course, and the winger Doug Holden.

Holden signed for Bolton in 1948, but, as with many of the young players at Burnden Park, National Service intervened and he did not make his first League appearance, against Liverpool, until 1951. Towards the end of the decade he achieved international recognition, winning five England caps. Remarkably, he would also contest another FA Cup Final in 1964, but this time wearing a Preston North End shirt. Tommy Banks says of a player he knew throughout his career at Bolton: "He was a most under-rated player. Many others in the team were the ones who were talked about by the supporters, but those that played with him knew what a good footballer he was."

Bill Ridding
and the
Backroom Staff

T HROUGHOUT the bulk of this era, the manager was Bill Ridding, and his proud boast that his 1958 Cup-winning side had been assembled for £110 – eleven signing-on fees of £10 – has entered football folklore. Sadly, it also underlined what was to be a serious weakness in the club in the early Sixties when the abolition of the maximum wage and the break-up of the team of the late Fifties saw the beginning of the struggle that was to lead to relegation and the football wilderness.

Ridding's association with Wanderers began in 1946 when he was appointed trainer. His own playing career had been prematurely curtailed at the age of 22 through a double cartilage injury after spells as a centre-forward for Tranmere Rovers and both Manchester United and City.

When he arrived at Burnden Park, the manager was Walter Rowley, a man whose playing career had ended at Wanderers as a wing-half or centre-half. Injury ended his playing days in May 1925 and then he worked his way through the backroom ranks, starting out as coach to the Reserves. By the time war broke out, he was first-team coach. He resigned due to ill health in October 1950 after serving the club in various guises for 38 years.

Bert Gregory's association with Wanderers, that was to last for more than thirty years, began in 1944 when he was asked by Rowley to make a sign reading, 'Spectators Not Allowed To Trespass.' He was paid £5, was suitably impressed by the manager's generosity, and was on hand to do more odd jobs around the stadium before finally being offered a full-time position. Only Nat Lofthouse has had a longer association with the club.

He said: "Walter Rowley had a vision to make Bolton Wanderers second to none, not just on the playing side but the backroom staff as well. He used to tell me he had great plans for the club when the war was over. He offered me £5 a week, which was more than in my old job and said I was my own boss and could start when I wanted."

Ridding was officially appointed secretary-manager of the Wanderers in February 1951. It ended three months of uncertainty when a number of alternative names were being bandied about and was in keeping with the club's tradition of appointing from within their own staff. Given that his successor, sixteen years later, would be Nat Lofthouse, it was a policy that was to continue. The new manager spoke of being anxious to justify the faith the directors had placed in him and his hope that he could retain the players' confidence in his judgment and impartiality. He stressed that the club's future success and well being was of the utmost importance to him.

Whether he succeeded in keeping the players' respect is a difficult question. This was a time when the club held all the power and the players were at their mercy. As Tommy Banks wryly notes, the pendulum has swung the other way in today's game. Probably no manager working under the constraints which Ridding faced from the directors above, and the power he wielded over the players below him, could ever win over the respect of the playing squad completely. Talking to some of those who played at this time the phrase "he was all right" probably best sums up the dressing-room mood.

For Ridding, his training role was now over, but he had won international recognition in that capacity as the trainer to England in the 1950 World Cup in Brazil. His new responsibilities were to be far different to anything modern managers would recognise. He was one of the last of the old school of secretary-managers and was now never to be seen in a tracksuit, working with the players. That job was left to the trainers. Rather he acted as the link between directors and team. Amazingly, he did not have the last word on team selection. That fell to the directors as well.

Eddie Hopkinson remarks: "Ridding was the manager of the club rather than the team. He wasn't daft enough to think he was the world's best coach and he wasn't. He was best at administration like sorting out the travel arrangements, organising things generally and booking the hotels. He made sure everything was laid on for us and everything ran as smooth as silk."

And he explained: "Ridding picked the team, but not without the consent of the board. Those were the terms on which he got the job. A lot of the time it was just rubber-stamped, but if they didn't like the selection, the directors could change it. The worse we were doing, the more interference you got. I remember one director sending a message to Roy Hartle that he needed to mark the opposing winger a bit tighter. This was a guy with Sunday league experience telling a senior professional like Roy. That was the sort of thing you'd get. Most of the directors were frustrated footballers and they wanted to be the manager. So they got a manager in who would do as they wished."

His dealings with the manager were no better than OK and Hopkinson remembers a couple of arguments over contracts. When the maximum wage was lifted, Hopkinson told the manager to his face that it would be the downfall of the club. All the clubs in Lancashire met to establish an artificial maximum wage that would have seen players get a rise from £20 during the season and £17 in summer to £30 and £25 respectively. It did not last because Manchester City quickly broke ranks to sign a player above the new limits. At this time Wanderers were the First Division side and City were in the Second. It was a clear indication of where the power in the game was shifting.

Tommy Banks has his own favourite anecdote to sum up the workings of the Bolton directors of his day. It may be apocryphal, but it is certainly worth telling anyway. The player himself swears it came from an impeccable source. He relates how Bolton were playing away to Preston North End and were in their change strip of red. Led by Tom Finney, in majestic form, the home side were having the best of it and by half-time were 3-0 up and coasting. A note from a director arrived in the Bolton dressing-room congratulating all the lads on playing so well. As Banks says derisively, the guy had mistaken Preston North End for his own club – and that was typical.

Banks adds: "Ridding was all right, but he wasn't a football man. The directors were the mad part. They weren't football men either. They were in business. Yet they were getting involved in the team and things they knew nothing about. I used to get into shouting matches over it."

He remembers that at the end of the season, the club used to regularly go on a tour abroad where the players would play three or four matches and earn £2 a day for their trouble. On the playing front there would be around thirteen players, the manager and trainer. Yet the party was swelled by another 26 directors and their wives, who he claims were each on £5 a day. He sees it as an example of the profligacy that swallowed up the revenues being generated by the club while there was no money for players or improvements to the ground. It is an issue that still rankles with the player.

Malcolm Barrass had been at the club since signing amateur forms in 1944 and he was signed by Joe Mercer for Sheffield

United in September 1956. It was not a happy departure and the player himself, even after more than forty years, is circumspect in discussing the events surrounding his move. "My relationship with Ridding was not the best. I had intimated I was willing to go, although it is possible I made a mistake. There were a lot of things. Wanderers was only a football team and I was still playing football after I went and I was good to those who paid my wages. However, I always have happy memories of Bolton Wanderers and if I had my time again, I wouldn't change a thing. The club must have had one of the best dressing-rooms. There might have been the occasional words, but in the main there was a great spirit."

'Circumspect' is not a word associated with Banks and he believes the loss of Barrass highlighted the shortsighted approach of the club and their unwillingness to countenance any criticism from within. "Transferring Malcolm Barrass broke his heart. He wasn't a 'yes man' and he had his own ideas. He was a good footballer with a good footballing brain. Why he never finished up in football when his playing days were over I will never know. When I first got into the side, if the winger got past me, then Malcolm was there. He was a gem to me. He was to everybody." In fact, after his footballing career was over, Barrass became a sales representative, although he did some coaching in non-League football.

The chief coach throughout this period was George Taylor with trainer Bert Sproston and assistant coach Roger Hunt. It was Taylor who was considered the visionary and Bert Gregory, for one, believes Ridding got much of the credit for the team's performance that should have gone to Taylor, a man who declared himself unavailable for the manager's job because he wished to continue with his coaching role. Banks calls him "the football brains at the club."

Taylor served Wanderers for more than fifty years as player, coach and scout. He had captained England Schoolboys before signing as a professional for Bolton, making his League debut in

April 1931 against Blackpool. He played his last game in 1945 before joining the coaching staff. He left in 1967, when he was awarded a testimonial to mark his devoted service to the club.

Bizarrely, Hopkinson recounts how Taylor rarely saw the first team play. Having spent the week at training and discussing tactics, his scouting role meant he was invariably required elsewhere come the day of the match. If the team had lost, he would ask the senior players what went wrong. It certainly highlights the limitations on coaching at this time, even though in many ways, Bolton were considered innovative.

He adds: "George Taylor was a wonderful man and he was astute enough to figure out what had happened in the game by his talk with us on Monday. We worked out how the goals were conceded and what we should be doing. He never swore or lost his temper and had a great enthusiasm for the game. He never lost that and he was in his fifties when I joined. He had his own ideas on how a wing-half should play, and was more a defender in outlook than an attacker. He had a great insight for the game and I can't remember anyone arguing with him. He was ahead of his time."

Ian Greaves believes the game is fundamentally the same today as it was when he played, although there is now more science involved. In his day, Manchester United rarely talked tactics. Matt Busby picked the side and they went out and played. It was the teams poorer in resources and playing power who relied more on giving themselves an edge through tactics and training methods. It is for this reason he has the highest regard for the coaching staff in this era and for Taylor in particular.

He remembers seeing the Wanderers' coaches in action and being impressed. George Taylor he knows was the key figure. A day spent sharing training facilities with the Bolton players gave him a rare insight into how another team prepares. The United players had the use of the pitches in the morning and Bolton were taking over for the afternoon session. What was revealed was a remarkable coaching session which showed how well organised Bolton were for the time.

Greaves recalls: "I knew many of the Bolton lads and stayed behind to watch them train. All we were used to doing at Old Trafford was running around the pitch. We weren't given any footballs to use until the last ten minutes, when we went and had a kickaround at the back of the stand. This was the fabulous Manchester United training. When we watched Bolton we couldn't believe it. They were running and training with the ball at their feet, then kicking it up for others to head it. The training was organised and concentrated on skills. Within a few years everybody got in on the act. Bolton were ahead of their day on that score. It took the Hungarians to wake everybody else up when they came over and showed us we weren't the best in the world and had been complacent."

Tommy Banks, though, remembers more than the tactics. He says the training kit which the players were expected to use was a disgrace. The players were given the same shirt from Monday to Friday, unlike at other clubs such as Everton where there was a clean strip every day. It might have saved on the Wanderers' laundry bill but Banks believed it was a ridiculous situation and was not backward in telling the powers-that-be as much.

Nat Lofthouse recalls Taylor making sure he kept his feet on the ground after his England debut against Yugoslavia in 1950, where he scored twice. The success was in danger of going to his head. The very next time Bolton lost, though, Lofthouse recalls being ordered in on Monday morning even though it was traditionally a day off for the players. He was to receive the biggest dressing-down of his career. Any ideas the player might have had about his self-importance were quickly dispelled. Taylor finished with the words which have always stayed with him: "You can do three things. You can run, shoot and head. You couldn't trap a bag of washing. So don't get fancy."

Roy Hartle cites Taylor and Sproston as major influences on

his career. They were there when he arrived as a 16-year-old amateur and were still there at the finish of his career. They had the day-to-day job of dealing with the players. "I think their strengths were being able to motivate the same players year after year after year. They also had a knack of never being any different. Irrespective of who you are, you must have good and bad days. During training they always appeared to be the same. I found them extremely good."

Concerning Ridding, the player who was heavily involved in the Professional Footballers' Association (PFA), eventually serving on the executive, says only: "He was all right. I have nothing against him."

Given modern training methods and kit, Hartle believes the players of his age could compete in the modern game. For a start, 10lbs could be taken off with modern boots, socks and pads and that would have an effect. He recalls that while the modern player can call on a whole range of experts for diet and fitness, the Bolton players in his day had nothing. After training, nobody questioned what the players were doing or where they were going.

Gordon Taylor remembers his dealings with Ridding with some affection. He was a man for whom he had enormous respect, but getting money out of him was never easy. When it came to on-the-field matters, his team talks were simplicity itself. Taylor recalls advice along the lines of "make sure you get your crosses in, keep your chips up and your ground passes low". That, as far as tactics from the manager went, was it.

As a former secretary at the club it was the business side of affairs where Ridding reigned. He made no secret of his belief that the abolition of the maximum wage would be the death knell of the game. As general secretary of the PFA, Taylor, for one, is delighted that prediction was wildly wrong. It was only for the traditional East Lancashire clubs that it spelt hard times.

Taylor remembers: "He was a wonderful old-time manager. A

man of his era. He was the sort of manager who, if you went in for a wage increase, would show you the list of free transfer players available and make you feel very grateful that you were in a job. He was used to the time of the maximum wage where clubs had big squads and management was very much in a dominant position."

He recalls two particular anecdotes that sum up Ridding's approach to parting with money. The first concerns his home Cup debut against Tottenham Hotspur, when he went in to ask for a pair of complementary tickets. Ridding asked who they were for and Taylor explained that they were for his parents. Ridding's reply was: "If your mum and dad won't pay to watch you, how can you expect anybody else to." He didn't get the tickets.

On another occasion the team were travelling to London for a game against Tottenham Hotspur in 1964. It was to prove the relegation season, but a win would have saved Bolton. On the train, Ridding announced that instead of the usual bonus of £2 for a draw and £4 for a win there would be a £10 win bonus if the side could beat Spurs. Taylor continues: "He had a short finger that he said had been shot off in the war, but the lads said he got it pulled off in a heated transfer deal. So when he went down the train holding up his hands to show how much we were on, Francis Lee, who even at that age was already as cheeky as ever, asked whether it was £10 or only £9 10s we were being offered." As they didn't win they'll never know the answer for sure.

Ridding saw the club through some of the best of times and then, with the abolition of the maximum wage and the difficulty of competing with city clubs with greater resources, he had the unenviable job of trying to keep Bolton from slipping out of the top flight with limited money at his disposal. As well as selling on some of the stalwarts of the club he was forced to mortgage the future by selling some of the brighter talent coming through the junior sides. A source of players that had served Bolton so well in the past.

He had always shared the popular desire to see the club at the top and fulfilled his pledge to work towards that end with the co-operation of the directors and the supporters. Towards the end, though, a disgruntled section of fans demanded change as Bolton slipped from the lofty heights they had enjoyed in the Fifties.

Finally it all got too much and the man who was a qualified physiotherapist and chiropodist left in August 1968 to set up his own physiotherapy business. He was to work for Lancashire County Cricket Club in the same capacity. At the time of his departure he was second only to Matt Busby at Manchester United as the League's longest-serving manager. He died in September 1981, aged 70.

In a simple epitaph Lofthouse remarked that any manager who had taken his side to two FA Cup Finals and won one had not done too bad a job. Although by the end he had lost the confidence of the supporters, few can doubt the sincerity of his words on taking up the appointment. In difficult circumstances he had always strived to put the well-being and success of the club first.

The Fifties Dawn:
1951 to 1954

THE dawn of the Fifties saw Bolton in fine form and in the early seasons of the decade they were challenging for the League, though in truth the players never really got close to getting their hands on the £100-a-man bonus that went with the silverware. It did mean, though, that the days of keeping a weather eye on the relegation dogfight were over for the time being.

Tommy Banks has his own view on Bolton's championship aspirations in the Fifties and he reveals he never really believed the team would win the League. "It was a hard league with a lot of good football being played and unlike nowadays more strength in depth. I remember once playing Huddersfield Town in the last match of the season and they were already relegated and they beat us 3-1. We were always a good home team, helped by a one-yard drop from one side of the pitch to the other. We didn't have a good away record, though."

Bolton enjoyed an unbeaten start to the 1951-52 season, going four games undefeated and enjoying the rare luxury of being top of the table, although the visit of Manchester United was expected to put paid to that lofty status. Bolton have never won the League title in their history, but although it was early days the supporters had the confidence a new season brings.

There were, though, already those who at the start of the Fifties were giving voice to a complaint that has dogged Wanderers since. The talk on the terraces was on the need to invest in new players to augment the home-grown talent that filled the Bolton ranks. In the pubs and mills they were all agreed that one or two big money signings might be the difference between being serious challengers for the title and lifting the coveted trophy itself. It was to prove a desire often repeated in the decades since – and largely unfulfilled.

It was not just the view of the supporters. Tommy Banks firmly believes if the club had spent more then they would have done far better. However, they rarely wanted to buy and he concedes that in many ways they didn't need to because there were still talented players coming through the club's own ranks, many of whom had been recruited from local leagues.

However, as a man involved with both United and Wanderers, Ian Greaves believes that although old Bolton players like Banks may wonder what happened to the money generated at Wanderers during this time, he is of the opinion that there was never the resources there that people imagined. He feels it was because Bolton couldn't buy that they assembled their famous Fifties team that had cost only £110, eleven players on a £10 signing-on fee. When he has his regular meeting with Banks and some of the other Bolton players of the era, it will no doubt be a debate to resolve over a friendly pint or two. Can't buy or won't buy? It is a question the fans have debated for decades and is a bone of contention that recurred throughout the Fifties.

Greaves says that while everybody remembers the occasional big gate for a key Cup-tie or the visit of a crowd-pulling side like Manchester United, these were very much one-offs. When the calculations are done over a season, the crowds averaged much less. It was a different story at Old Trafford where Greaves once overheard a conversation in which a United director expressed his concern to Sir Matt Busby that the crowd numbers were down to only 52,000. This was when the Reserves could get 22,000 watching. United were buying players for £30,000 when Wanderers were looking to recruit from the lower divisions for £3,000.

Certainly Malcolm Barrass concurs, arguing that the supporters turned out only for the big matches. Teams like Charlton and Portsmouth might have been riding high in the League at times, but they failed to catch the imagination of the soccer-going public in the town.

The particular animosity that Wanderers fans feel for Manchester United is well known, but in passing Greaves also mentions that the gripe that, as the Old Trafford fortunes soar and the club's financial clout increases it is to the detriment of today's game, misses the point. He reckons it was always the case. He points out that Sir Alex Ferguson is doing the same as Busby did in making the most of the cash at his disposal. In his view people tend to have short memories.

Bolton did, of course, raid the bank account, but not often. The only big-money signing of its day that Banks highlights as the exception to the rule was the arrival of Harold Hassall. And he was a local lad, from Tyldesley, close to the town, who had managed to slip the Burnden Park scouting system's net. He was spotted by Huddersfield Town and signed in 1946. He made his League debut two seasons later. While at Town he won four caps before transferring to Wanderers in January 1952, in a deal worth £27,000. He was to win another England cap the following year.

An injury on New Year's Day in 1955, against Chelsea, ended his playing career and he went into teaching, buoyed by the proceeds of a benefit game that attracted 20,000 fans. His great claim to fame was that at Huddersfield Town he once saved a penalty by Tom Finney after he had gone into goal when the 'keeper was injured.

However much money Manchester United might have generated in whichever decade, at the start of the Fifties the Bolton fans must have been reaching for their lucky charms because that old jinx was soon to be working again. Bolton may have been unbeaten, but United also arrived at Burnden Park having not lost. It was the visitors whose run was to end and for the moment those local Bolton lads were plenty good enough for the task in hand. The only goal came courtesy of Lofthouse, who, after being played onside by an opponent, was happy to make the most of the opportunity. A Moir cross had taken a deflection off a United player. Attempts to get the referee to consult a linesman and overturn the decision fell on deaf ears, to the relief of the home fans.

Chances were few and far between with the defenders of both sides having the upper hand, but United were to rue two good chances wasted by Rowley. When Barrass targeted teams that could pack Burnden, United were top of the list and that was confirmed with a 55,477 attendance that set a new post-war League record for the ground. Not since the Cup-tie with Stoke City in 1946, that ended in disaster, had the 50,000 barrier been broken. For Manchester United the defeat was a temporary blip as they went on to win the title.

For the home side the unbeaten run ended at Tottenham Hotspur on September 8, but it was a slump in form that began on Boxing Day and saw Bolton go seven games without a win that ended any hopes of a title challenge. Still, fifth place in the division was an improvement on the previous campaign when they finished eighth. The post-war days of potential relegation, for the moment at least, appeared to be a thing of the past.

After being high in the table for two seasons, Bolton's League form slumped, but did the fans care? Not a bit of it. This was the year when the Cup took precedence. The games that had the supporters on the edge of their seats were for the chance of a trip to Wembley rather than any hopes of lifting the League championship trophy.

There was, though, a holiday treat in store for more than 45,000 who dragged themselves away from the festivities for a 1952 Christmas Day fixture with Arsenal. Ten goals in a marvellous match of entertaining football was their reward. The only disappointment was that victory went to the London side.

Moir had the chance to put Bolton ahead inside a minute before shortly afterwards putting Wanderers in the lead by converting a neat move. It did not deter Arsenal, who came back quickly with double-international Arthur Milton equalising after comprehensively beating two defenders. It was the visitors who enjoyed a half-time lead after a terrific shot from Cliff Holton.

After the interval the floodgates opened with Arsenal clinching goals from Don Roper and Jimmy Logie as the visitors took control. Bolton, however, did not capitulate and answered like with like, Lofthouse quickly scoring. When Arsenal added two more, it looked all over, but Bolton responded with second goals for both Lofthouse and Moir. With only five minutes remaining, Bolton won a penalty-kick, but Jack Kelsey in the Arsenal goal palmed the ball away and Bolton then had too much to do. It was, though, great entertainment.

An interested spectator was Roy Hartle, who watched with the reserve team in the stand. After the game he went into the dressing-room because the reserve side were planning to travel with the first-team squad to London the following day because it was traditional to reverse the Christmas Day fixture on Boxing Day. When he checked the team sheet he was down to make his first-team debut at Highbury. He was to be disappointed, though, because after travelling down, the match was postponed. The team went to watch Fulham play instead.

Unusually for Bolton, Hartle wasn't a local lad or even from the North West. He came from a village just outside Bromsgrove in the West Midlands and was approached by a scout for Wanderers after playing in a cup match for Bromsgrove Rovers. He opted for Bolton rather than local club Aston Villa because his father advised there would be less pressure on him and it was the local boys who got the most flak.

He remembers his first trip to the town in 1947. "I came from a small village and this was the first time I had left home and I felt absolutely terrified as I arrived in Manchester and caught a train to Bolton. It was such a big industrial place. I was also aware that Bolton Wanderers were a top club. I went into the army in 1950 because I had no choice and I think that probably made the difference to my career; from being an average player to more than that." Among his army colleagues was one Tommy Banks, who had already made his first-team debut for Wanderers, in 1948.

The postponed game against Arsenal was only a temporary setback for Hartle as he got his chance against Charlton on New Year's Day. A 2-1 home defeat was not an ideal start. but he kept his place despite the reverse, playing in 24 League and Cup games. In fact, he appeared in every round of the Cup up to Wembley. With the Final less than a month away, Bolton played Sheffield Wednesday at Hillsborough and Hartle admits he didn't have a good game. He was shocked by the outcome, though.

"I have tried to put it out of my mind. I still can't believe what happened. Having played all the Cup rounds, I was dropped for the Final. I did get a Cup Final medal, but it didn't mean anything when I sat watching the game. I didn't play another first-team game until the start of the 1955-56 season. It was the biggest disappointment of my career along with not being capped for England, although many said I should have been." Indeed, he is considered one of the unluckiest full-backs never to have pulled on the England jersey.

In an ironic coincidence, the other full-back from the semi-final, George Higgins, also failed to make the Final. Having joined from Blackburn Rovers in July 1951, the Scot made forty League appearances in 1951-52, but the following year lost his place to Ralph Banks, who ran out at Wembley.

These were also days that pre-date any idea of man management. A player's sensibilities were of no concern. There was no comforting word for the young player facing the hammer blow of being dropped. Hartle says: "There was nothing like having a quiet word to break the news or someone putting their arm around you. It was pinned on the notice board. I remember going in and not daring to look at the team sheet. When I did, it confirmed my worst fears and I wasn't in the side."

Sometimes a cavalier approach to players can backfire. Eddie Hopkinson would eventually play in a club record 519 League games and be the England goalkeeper on fourteen occasions, but his services were nearly lost to Wanderers. In 1950, the 15-year-old Hopkinson signed on for the club on their ground staff.

He recounts the tale: "When I went to the ground there was nobody there to meet me. I'd travelled from my home in Royton to Rochdale, then to Manchester and on to Bolton. I was disgusted that there was nobody there, so I went home and never bothered. George Taylor rang me to ask what was the matter and I told him. I was only fifteen and it was a big shock to my ego that there was no one to meet me."

Another player who arrived on the same day as Hopkinson was also to make his mark at Burnden during the Fifties. When he ran out against Wolves in October 1951, aged fifteen years and 267 days, Ray Parry was the youngest player to appear in the First Division. The former England schoolboy had only six games in the Reserves before being given his chance in the first team, although it would not be until 1953-54 that he became firmly established in the side at inside-forward. International honours came as the decade ended when he won the first of two caps in 1959, against Northern Ireland.

Hopkinson, meanwhile, signed for Oldham Athletic and was only sixteen when he played in three Third Division North games as an amateur in 1951-52. The footballing fates were to ensure his return to Wanderers. He was also working as a trainee draughtsman with a company owned by the chairman of Oldham. Because he was only on amateur forms, his contract automatically lapsed when the season ended and suddenly the youngster was in demand.

"Manchester United, Manchester City and Everton were all interested and made contact," he recalls, "but so too did George Taylor. He was a man I had a lot of respect for and he was an astute coach. He came round to the house and left me the forms if I wanted to sign. I decided to think about it and talk to my father, but in the end I opted to go to Bolton Wanderers."

At the company where he worked the boss called him "un-British" when he read in the newspaper he was joining Bolton after being given his chance with Oldham Athletic. When Hopkinson explained that nobody from the Latics had been in touch, he received an apology. It was to be Oldham's loss and Wanderers' gain. Hopkinson signed pro forms with Bolton on his seventeenth birthday in November 1952, although he was not to break into the first team until the 1956-57 season.

On the field Bolton had already experienced a taste of the disappointing League form that was to see the side finish in fourteenth place in the table in their Cup Final season of 1952-53. It came early in the calendar when Portsmouth were the visitors and, to the dismay of the nearly 30,000, present completely outclassed the home side. Bolton had created some good early chances, but squandered them and were to pay a heavy price for such profligacy as they went down 5-0. With a neat passing game, Portsmouth opened up the Bolton defence at will. The goal of the game saw Dale, the outside-left, twice appear to lose control before outpacing Barrass and passing inside for Harris to drive the shot home. The home fans were convinced the last goal by Phillips was offside. It hardly mattered.

There was better news, and what many hoped would be a good omen for the Cup Final, when Blackpool were the visitors early in the new year. Four-nil to the Wanderers. What would the fans have given for that scoreline when they visited the Twin Towers? The victory was all the more surprising in that it came on the back of three defeats in a row for Bolton. However, the home side's cause had been helped by a knee injury to Blackpool centre-forward Stan Mortensen, who retired after less than two minutes. Bolton had blooded some of their reserve team, but they coped well. Moir scored the first after the 'keeper was unsighted by defenders, and a hat-trick for Wheeler in the second half secured the points.

This was another of those games where the conditions were a great leveller. This suited Bolton. Indeed, during his own playing days at Burnden Park, Gordon Taylor heard rumours that it was not unknown for the ball to be watered. And with the pitch being built on old barrels and cotton bales, it had the most cambered surface in the League. As was remarked on in the Blackpool game, the home side also possessed players more willing than the opposition to put their limbs on the line.

With less than a month to the Final, Nat Lofthouse showed he was in fine goalscoring form with a hat-trick against Sunderland, including a penalty. A holiday crowd of 34,862 crammed into Burnden Park for the Easter game and with a place at Wembley secure, the crowd were in confident mood and even a couple of easy misses by Lofthouse were forgiven early on in the sure knowledge that goals would eventually come. A 5-0 win showed their confidence was not misplaced. Two Lofthouse goals within four minutes of the second half set them on the way to victory. The centre-forward completed his hat-trick with a volley from a Holden centre.

However, the April 3 win was to be the last until a victory over Newcastle in the last League game of the season. Lofthouse was among many at the time who argued that the gap between the Cup semi-final on March 21 and the Final in May was too long. The argument was that when players have Wembley on their minds, then their League form suffers. They are also frequently haunted by fear of picking up an injury that would jeopardise their Wembley place. His view was that there should be less time between the semi-final and the Final.

On The Road to Wembley

IT WAS an inauspicious start to the FA Cup campaign that was to end at Wembley with the third-round tie at home to Fulham postponed because of fog. Throughout the week building up to the match on January 10, 1953, it had been the ice-bound pitch that posed the biggest threat, but on the day the referee could not be seen after he had walked twenty yards from the touchline. Wanderers may have traditionally revelled in difficult conditions, but even they could not contemplate playing in such dense fog.

It was the following Wednesday when the match finally got under way and despite it being a midweek fixture, more than 32,000 filed through the turnstiles to see the home side's attacking flair carry them through 3-1. However, only the most optimistic would have regarded this as a Cup-winning performance and it was the visitors who opened the scoring with a goal from former Manchester United star, Charlie Mitten. Bolton replied when Lofthouse profited from a skilful Langton dribble to bring the sides level and then the centre-forward provided the centre for Holden to give Bolton the lead. With three minutes remaining Moir settled the issue and gave the scoreline a flattering look which Bolton scarcely deserved.

Florence Brandwood was, of course, at the game and although it wasn't Wanderers at their best, she was pleased her favourite player had been on form. Not Nat Lofthouse, although he was popular. She believes Lofthouse owes a lot to the skills of Bobby Langton, who made so many of his goals. "Langton was my favourite because he was such a good, skilful player. There were rarely any worries about offside with Langton because he always got to the by-line for his crosses."

Langton began his career at Blackburn Rovers before the war, but soon after football resumed when peace returned he was transferred to Preston North End where he won the first of his eleven England caps. He was signed by Bolton for what was then a club record fee of £20,000 in November 1949. He left after the 1953 Final.

The win against Fulham set up an epic tie with Notts County that needed three matches to resolve and was shrouded in controversy. If Wanderers had exited from the Cup here, there could have been few complaints from the fans because both sides had chances to clinch it and whoever went through could claim to have had the footballing gods on their side.

In the first tie at Burnden Park, County took the lead with a ferocious shot by McPherson in the first half. Thereafter it was all Bolton pressure with the visitors defending valiantly. Lofthouse brought the scores level, but the home side could not find the winner in a game dominated by a strong wind that made football a lottery. Then, in the dying moments, Langton had the chance to clinch the game, but could only watch in frustration as his shot hit the bar. A crowd of more than 40,000 generated gate receipts of £5,739.

And so to Nottingham where County twice took the lead, but Bolton always came back. A Langton pass set up Moir for the first equaliser and then it was Moir again who kept Wanderers in contention when he fired home from a pass by Hassall. In extra-time Lofthouse appeared to have won it for the visitors and the Bolton players and supporters were certain he had. He looked to have been played onside when the ball hit a defender's legs, but despite protests, the referee disallowed the goal.

There was controversy again when the teams met at Hillsborough, but this time the decision went with Lofthouse, although there were many who felt the only goal in the match should not have been allowed. It was a typical effort by the powerful centre-forward who bundled 'keeper and ball over the line with a robust challenge. The linesman certainly had his flag raised and the County players were convinced that a foul should have been awarded, but the goal stood. Until that moment County had never been in arrears in five hours of football and could consider themselves unlucky.

Malcolm Barrass recalls an incident when a long ball was played through and everybody stopped except himself, the County centre-forward, and Bolton 'keeper Stan Hanson. "I set off in pursuit and it went through my mind that I was chasing a Cup medal. That was when being in the Cup was really brought home. Hanson blocked the shot and I cleared it. County should have knocked us out. We were lucky when we drew at Burnden and luckier still down at their place."

He believes Wanderers had the luck that was going with the controversial Lofthouse goal and another incident when there was a dispute over whether the ball was over the line. In the dying minutes a County player had the easiest of chances to equalise from about ten yards out, but he managed to mishit it and the ball bounced and rolled towards the line. Roy Hartle belted it the length of the field while some County players claimed it had gone over the line, but as the debate raged, the referee blew for time. Surviving such a tough early round in such circumstances gave the players the belief that this might indeed be their year.

Luton were always going to be an easier prospect and so it proved, although on the day the weather looked as if it might play its part. Volunteers were recruited to clear the pitch of snow so the game could get under way. Once the match started, the visitors always had the edge and a Lofthouse header decided proceedings after the 'keeper had committed himself to a cross and then found himself stranded.

The sixth round saw another away tie and again it was opposition from the lower divisions. In the great tradition of the Cup, Gateshead rose to the occasion and the Third Division North players relished the chance to harass their illustrious opposition. Bolton struggled to find any rhythm on a small playing surface, although their defence always looked secure. The reliable combination of a Langton cross converted by a Lofthouse header was enough to book a semi-final place and keep alive the centre-forward's remarkable record of scoring in every round.

On a fine and sunny day, the stage was set for an epic semi-final at Maine Road. Moir won the toss for Bolton and opted to make Everton play into a bright sun. From the start it was Wanderers who dominated, forcing four corner-kicks in the first six minutes with Lofthouse already beginning to find the range with his goal attempts.

Eventually Bolton scored the goal for which they had worked so hard. Holden, on the wing, put in a centre but 'keeper O'Neill completely misjudged it and the ball swerved into the far corner of the net. The Everton centre-forward, Dave Hickson, had been involved in a ferocious battle with Barrass, the Bolton centre-half, in which no prisoners were taken and it was the forward who came off worse, retiring injured in the 25th minute, although he returned later with his head stitched and swathed in bandages.

Barrass remembers years later working as a sales representative and visiting a social club in Liverpool where a woman came up to him and said she was Dave Hickson's mother. Expecting a friendly chat, the former Bolton man was taken aback by the verbal assault he was on the receiving end of, fuelled by what had happened on the pitch all those years ago. When he returned a few weeks later, the woman came back and

Barrass was prepared for another onslaught, only to be told by the contrite woman "Our David says I have to apologise to you."

Bolton's second goal went to Moir after good work by Langton and Hassall. Lofthouse got the third when he headed the ball down, sprinted after it and angled a powerful shot into the far corner of the net. As the minutes ticked down to half-time, Lofthouse scored again and Everton squandered a chance to reduce the deficit when Clinton missed the penalty.

Lofthouse recalls being in the dressing-room at half-time with four goals to the good and the general feeling being that the team was on course for a big win. However, manager Bill Ridding warned against easing up, advising that if Wanderers could score four in the first half, then Everton were capable of doing the same in the second. The words were very nearly to prove prophetic as the Merseysiders staged an amazing fight back.

Barrass recalls that it was not a good game for the Everton 'keeper. "Jimmy O'Neill had a terrible match and made mistakes galore with the goals we got. The game was particularly special for me because it was at Maine Road, my dad's old ground and where I used to watch City as a lad many times. Just when we looked to have got the game won, the referee helped Everton back in. He awarded a free-kick just outside our box and I cleared the ball. Then he told them to take the kick again and it was in the back of the net. We weren't happy and it shook us up a bit. We had been cruising up until then."

Two headed goals for John Parker and a well-struck shot by captain Peter Farrell gave Bolton a scare and the fans tremendous excitement as the fortunes of the tie now swung in Everton's favour. Hickson had returned after injury but could still not get the better of Barrass, and Bell was also outstanding, but in the end Bolton were happy to hear the whistle, having booked a trip to Wembley for themselves and their ecstatic supporters.

Fred and Florence Guest were at the game and recall a really exciting match. With Bolton in control their confidence soared, but as Everton staged their fightback, it began to ebb. Florence says: "We had played brilliantly in the first half and it looked all over bar the shouting. By the end we were hanging on for grim death as suddenly they started winning possession and scoring goals. At the end, every Bolton fan was urging the referee to blow the whistle and we were anxiously looking at our watches, like Sir Alex Ferguson does at Manchester United."

The Guests explained how the whole town had been increasingly gripped by the excitement as their team progressed in the Cup. At their shop, people would stop and chat football. It was the talk of the town. Although to some it might seem strange, given it was "only a game", they said Bolton's success raised everybody's spirits.

For Roy Hartle it was the biggest game he had played in at that stage in his career and he can remember it passing so quickly that it was difficult to take it all in. It almost seems, he explained, like somebody else was playing. By the end, Bolton were hanging on by the skin of their teeth. There is another aspect of the game he remembers. "It appeared to me that Malcolm Barrass and the Everton centre-forward were kicking each other around the field. The ball seemed insignificant. Afterwards I sat in the dressing-room, overawed."

Tom Hodgkinson had been unable to get a ticket to the match and listened to the drama on the radio. Like those around him he could not believe Everton had come back from 4-0 down and were close to grabbing the equaliser. It was, he says, a real nail-biter, but then in more than fifty years of watching the team he has come to accept that Wanderers get more than their fair share of nail-biting matches.

Florence Brandwood had watched the game gripped with excitement, but now she was in no doubt what she had to do. She went straight round to Burnden Park and to the gate where the Cup Final tickets would go on sale the following morning and where fans were already beginning to queue. She sent her husband home with instructions to bring three 3s 6d postal orders and began to prepare for a long, cold night outside the ground.

The following day, the wait was worthwhile. She had Cup Final tickets for herself, husband Harry and young son David.

She recalls: "It wasn't all plain sailing, even though I had been waiting all night. Some people were trying to buy too many. A man in front of me asked for a dozen, but then the manager Bill Ridding intervened and said he couldn't have them. He pointed me out and said he knew for a fact I had been there all night and made sure I got my tickets."

Everything was now set for the Final, but a League match against Tottenham was to have dire consequences for Wanderers' Cup dreams, although few could guess it at the time. Eric Bell was injured in a 3-2 defeat. Wing-half Bell began his professional career with Manchester United, but was quickly recruited by Bolton and had only this season broken into the first team where he was in irrepressible form. The extent of his injury has long been the subject of much speculation among fans.

As the club tried to play down the seriousness of the damage, Bert Gregory had an insider's view and knew it was worse than was being claimed. Bell was to go on to play in the Final after declaring himself fit. Gregory, for one, is in no doubt it was a mistake. "He shouldn't have played. He was declared fit to play but he wasn't. He lasted only eighteen minutes in the Final and then we were effectively down to ten men."

Despite the depth of talent at full-back, the injury to Bell meant Tommy Banks entertained an outside chance of running out at Wembley. A local reporter had told him that Bell's injury was more serious than at first thought and a good game could see him in. The opportunity never came.

He also might have got the nod over his brother Ralph, who was ten years his senior. In the end, the decision was to go with experience rather than youth and Tommy was to be a spectator while his brother took centre stage with the unenviable task of marking Stanley Matthews. His mother prophetically told Tommy not to worry because his turn would come. It did five years later.

Broken Dreams: The Matthews Final

WITH a month to go to the big match on May 2, 1953, the groundswell of opinion that this should be the occasion when Stanley Matthews finally got his winners' medal was already starting to build and Bolton players and fans had only to glance at the national newspapers to see how the idea of a "Stanley Matthews Final" was being built up. The player himself was inundated with fan mail and good wishes on his third attempt at being on a winning side at Wembley.

The Bolton players had decided to stay at home rather than go to an out-of-town training camp in the build up to the Final. They worked out at Burnden before, on the Thursday before the match, heading for Hendon in North London, where the squad was to be based. The players were calm and confident on the morning of the match. Lofthouse recalls that the key instruction from manager Bill Ridding was to try to dictate play.

The day before leaving Bolton, though, there had been a bad omen for Malcolm Barrass, who was not particularly superstitious. It was a moment he still remembers and it is not something that has happened before or since. Nor is it something he can explain. He said: "I came down the stairs and said to my wife that we would not win the Cup. Up to that moment I was full of confidence. I don't know what happened. It was just something hit me."

For Bert Gregory it was his first trip to Wembley and he recalls the wonderful experience of walking up Wembley Way on the day of the match. Everybody was happy and although he thought the Blackpool fans a bit snobbish, there was no trouble between rival supporters. Rather there was a party atmosphere.

The weather was perfect and the conditions ideal as the players lined up to be introduced to Prince Philip. The stadium was packed, of course, and Bolton were in a mood to ruin Matthews' big day. And within two minutes of the start they were in the lead with a goal by Nat Lofthouse from 25 yards out on the right, after a quick pass inside by Holden, although the shot was not as powerful as it might have been and George Farm in the Blackpool goal should have saved it. Lofthouse had now succeeded in the not inconsiderable feat of scoring in every round of the Cup. Blackpool settled, but the goal had given the Wanderers confidence and they worked hard to try to extend the lead.

The injury doubts about Bell were now confirmed. It meant an enforced change of positions with Langton moving to inside-left, Bell taking over from him at outside-left and Hassall dropping into the left-half position vacated by Bell. It was, however, to be Blackpool who scored next through Stan Mortensen, whose shot was helped by a Hassall deflection. They were not on level terms for long, though, as a 39th-minute goal for Moir gave Bolton a half-time lead. The general consensus was that it was a poor first half with nerves perhaps taking their toll.

Yet Lofthouse recalls an incident which he believes sums up the nature of the game in this era. At half-time, Mortensen shook his hand and congratulated him on scoring in every round. A piece of sportsmanship that it is hard to imagine being repeated halfway through a Cup Final in this day and age.

Bolton's workmanlike approach was giving them the edge over Blackpool's neater passing moves and in the 55th minute the injured Bell remarkably scored their third when he got his head to a Holden cross. That the Bolton man was able to get to the ball was, in the view of Eddie Hopkinson, nothing short of incredible.

Fred and Florence Guest had booked into the Russell Hotel on Russell Square in the heart of London and were making a weekend of the Final because Fred did a lot of business in London. Their daughter was not interested in the game, but had driven them to Wembley only to find herself surrounded by policemen eager to listen to the action unfold on the radio. With Bolton in a comfortable lead, a fellow guest at the Russell Hotel now tapped Florence on the shoulder and promised champagne back at the hotel. The celebrations were already being planned by the Bolton contingent. It was to prove premature.

Florence remembers Stanley Matthews delivering the cross that was to decide the contest from right in front of them. The player fell as he made contact, but the ball was still accurately delivered. Although it meant defeat, she can remember being mesmerised by the skill of the Blackpool winger dribbling the ball as only he could.

She said: "We had lost and it was all through Stanley Matthews. We were sorry to have lost, but Matthews was so popular and admired, we thought that if we had to be beaten we were glad it was Blackpool. We were good losers. If it had been another side I might have been more upset. And it was a Lancashire derby. We still went back and celebrated and when we opened the champagne, we toasted Stanley Matthews. It was Stan who had won."

Hopkinson, as befits a goalkeeper, has sympathy for Stan Hanson who was in goal for Wanderers. The 66th-minute goal by

Mortensen came when Hanson failed to hold a Matthews cross and the centre-forward pounced, pushing the ball just inside the post. The 'keeper had been with Wanderers since joining as a nineteen-year-old in 1935 and during the war was involved in the retreat from Dunkirk.

"I've read and talked about that game for the past forty odd years," says Hopkinson, "and it was quite remarkable, although Stanley Matthews only took part in the last twenty minutes. He had done bugger-all up until then. Hanson had a good pair of hands, but when he let a Matthews cross through and Mortensen knocked it in, that was the beginning of the end. I know Hanson was upset about the goal because he was normally so reliable. It was one of the few times he made a mistake and you could say it cost Bolton the Cup. I know he certainly felt that way."

Yet another verdict on a crucial turning point in the match is delivered by Tommy Banks, who was also watching from the sidelines. Although all are agreed on the significance of Bell's injury, the number of dramatic moments highlighted by the watching professionals is proof of what an exciting contest the game was. In Banks' view, Dougie Holden was Bolton's best player and was unlucky to have been penalised for a tackle in a dangerous position for Wanderers. It was to prove costly. Mortensen's shot from the free-kick, three yards outside the penalty area, beat the unsighted Hanson and provided Blackpool's equaliser.

Sitting on the touchline, a disappointed Roy Hartle remembers thinking that although he had missed out on getting on to the pitch for what might be the highlight of his football life, there was at least the consolation of the £25 win bonus because the team looked well on course for victory. Then it all went to pieces. He has no complaints about Bell declaring himself fit after his injury a few weeks earlier. As he says, many other players given the chance of a place in the Cup Final would have done the same. Crucially, though, it meant Bolton were down to ten men.

So just when it looked as if the Cup would be heading back to Bolton, the memorable events unfolded. The Mortensen goal capitalising on Hanson's mistake put the Seasiders back into contention at 3-2. Until this point, Matthews had been kept relatively quiet but with defenders tiring, particularly having to cover for the injured Bell, it was now that the veteran winger worked his magic and drew on all his vast experience. Suddenly the crosses started to be fired over and Bolton were under pressure. It was only a matter of time before Mortensen completed his hat-trick with that well-struck free-kick. The public may have dedicated the match to Matthews, but the player himself was in no doubt. As he said in his own book *The Stanley Matthews Story*: "Anyone who scores a hat-trick in a Cup Final is the man of the match."

Hartle recalls: "The thing I can remember was Stan. He was destroying everyone. I felt sorry for Ralph Banks who was struggling to deal with him. It was as though the thought had crossed Stan's mind that this was his last chance. If he didn't do it now, then that was the end."

Bolton were desperately struggling to hang on now and with only a few minutes left to play, it was their opponents who were going all out for the winner. With a minute to go, Matthews controlled the ball and raced away, beating two defenders as the crowd urged him on, although not the watching Florence Guest and the Bolton fans in the stand. The winger centred and Bill Perry netted the winning goal. Matthews had his medal and the Bolton players were left with only heartbreak.

In his book *Goals Galore* Lofthouse confesses: "When I reached the dressing-room I broke down for the first time since I was a boy and wept unashamedly. Even the champagne we had brought with us to Wembley tasted bitter."

Gregory had feared the worst when Bell was injured and the team was effectively down to ten men. They were being run off the park and tiredness took its toll. Matthews, who had been kept in check, now began to cut loose and as Gregory says, the rest is history.

He said: "The way we lost, it broke our hearts. I had to console the wife. It was all so depressing. Despite the result I did enjoy the occasion, though, because it was all so new to us. We went to the Café Royal for the banquet in the evening and the team was there. It was the best meal I had ever seen. There was one course after the other. The players were sorry they had lost, but they had a good excuse being down to ten men. They couldn't help it, but in the end we were second best. The thing was that Matthews never tired. He was always the fit man. That was the cause of our downfall."

Match day had not been a happy occasion for Florence Brandwood and it wasn't just the matter of Bolton losing. She was in hospital for a major operation. She had acquired tickets for the match and kept them until the last minute in the hope she might be released from hospital in time. Her pleas, though, were in vain. She jokes that she was the most popular person in the infirmary when news spread that she had three spare tickets.

She can remember only parts of the match. As she explained: "I put the disappointment of not being able to go to Wembley behind me and settled down to watch the match. When Lofty scored after two minutes – I fainted! They turned the television off after that because the nurse didn't want me to get too excited. When I came round I pleaded with them to put it back on and she relented, but I was warned if I got excited again it would be going off and staying off."

She remembers the heartbreak as the BBC commentator announced: "Yes, it's there. Perry has scored, Perry has scored number four, laid on by Stanley Matthews." It was the biggest disappointment in her fanatical devotion to Wanderers.

While others may rave about the excitement of the Final, from a professional players point of view Malcolm Barrass regards it as "a bloody awful game" because it was a match decided by mistakes and Bolton were far from blameless. Neither was the referee for giving the free-kick that wasn't, from which Mortensen scored. To cap the catalogue of errors, the centre-forward took advantage of a badly-formed defensive wall which broke. As Barrass says, Mortensen didn't need to swerve the ball. He just hit it straight.

Giving yet another perspective on why it all went wrong for Bolton, the defender highlights another key figure in the Blackpool revival to go alongside Matthews and Mortensen. He believes a turning point was the passing skills of Ernie Taylor, who began to provide the winger with a wonderful service. Early on, the Bolton defenders were successful at keeping Matthews quiet, but he was now getting perfect passes.

He adds: "It had been a harum-scarum Cup run and we were all glad to be at Wembley. We were all friends together and it is a good occasion to share. We all played our hardest on the field and then went for a pint with the Blackpool lads after. We might have been enemies on the pitch, but when the referee blew the final whistle we were all old pals again."

Matthews had vowed to himself after being on the losing side in the 1951 Final, and kicking the turf in desperation, that he would return one day. Now, as he said in his book, once the after-match furore was over and the Cup had been paraded around the ground and the interviews and photographs were completed, he changed, quietly left the dressing-room, and made his way back up the tunnel and on to the pitch.

"The vast stadium was now deserted. I walked to the spot where I had kicked the turf at the end of the 1951 Final, looked up in the sky, and held out the medal in the palm of my hand – it was the only way I could think of to show it to my father. As I held out my medal, the sun came from behind a small cloud and shone down on it. Standing there, a wonderful feeling of peace entered my mind and body. I felt that all the years from boyhood to manhood in football finished here. I had fulfilled my destiny."

For Tom Hodgkinson, now chairman of the Wanderers supporters' club, the match was a great disappointment, but proved the defining moment when Bolton Wanderers would play a huge part in his life. He had been unable to get a ticket for the game and joined neighbours who piled into the only house in the street with a television, to watch the match on the tiny screen.

"When we went 3-1 up there were celebrations in the house and there was a real party mood. We all thought it was over and done with. Then players started going down injured and the atmosphere became electric as Blackpool began to come back. As a teenager I was completely gutted at the end. I wouldn't have minded if it had gone into extra-time and given us something to cheer about. Everybody was devastated when Perry scored in the last minute."

The irrepressible Tommy Banks couldn't resist a quick word with the great Matthews who had so tormented his brother on the field in the dying stages of the game, and when the winger had returned from his reveries there was Banks. "I told Stan that we wouldn't have lost if I had played, but it never bothered Stan one little bit. He didn't care. He had his medal and he was never fazed anyway. I was a bit of a rabbit for him though. I don't know why, but I always had a fair game against him. He was still a ghost on the field though."

And Banks is happy to put an end to a popular myth among Bolton supporters that Matthews used to cry off games at Burnden, fearing the infamous gravel rash from one of his tackles. Sadly, it's nonsense. As the player says, Matthews wasn't afraid of anything or anyone on a football field.

At the after-match banquet, the captain, Willie Moir, felt the game had been lost because the match was five minutes too long and his players were exhausted by having run themselves into the ground. Certainly injuries took their toll with Bell a virtual passenger for much of the game and at various times Lofthouse and Ralph Banks also off the field receiving treatment. There was a feeling expressed that when Matthews began to weave his magic at the expense of Banks, there should have been a reshuffle with Banks swopping wings with the fitter and in-form Johnny Ball. Hindsight, of course, is a precise science.

Roy Hartle believes the result hastened the break-up of the 1953 side. For at least three of the players it probably brought an early departure from Bolton Wanderers as their top-flight careers were ended. "If you were a neutral or a Blackpool supporter, it must have been fantastic drama as Stanley Matthews pulled everybody everywhere, although as professionals we gave the Final to Mortensen. You can't score a hat-trick and not be man of the match."

The worst part for Hartle, though, was the return to Bolton to face the crowds from the Town Hall steps. That was when the bitter disappointment really sunk in as thousands turned out to cheer the players home, but they had nothing to show for their Wembley adventure. All taste for the civic dinner had gone.

Nearly fifty years on, the player who watched from the touchline now admits: "It is a terrible thing to say, but I was sat there thinking if I had been out there it would have been different. It might not have made any difference, of course. I might have even made things worse. But as a professional you think if only I could get out there and have a go."

Among the mass of bodies who crowded outside the Town Hall was Florence Brandwood, who, in order to get a good vantage point near the rails at the front, had arrived three hours before the bus brought the players. There was disappointment among the crowd, but also a sense that they needed to get behind the team to raise their spirits.

She said: "You could tell by looking at them how down they were, but we put on a right good welcome for them. It was a brilliant turnout and I only wish I could have got nearer to them, but at least I had a good view. After they went inside we began the walk home, talking about the match. We still couldn't believe how we managed to lose. It was a great shame."

Barrass was disappointed, and glad not to be staying in Bolton for too long after the homecoming as he departed with the England party on a tour of South America. What hurt him was disgruntled fans accusing the players of throwing it away. As he says: "Nobody throws a Cup Final away do they?"

The match itself was to have particularly poignant memories for the player as well. "For me it was a disaster. It was the last time I saw my father. He died that summer of a heart attack and he had come to the Final. I am happy that he saw me achieve everything I said I would do as a little lad. I played for England and in a Wembley Cup Final and he saw me do both. The only thing that was wrong was the England game was at Wembley and he would have wanted it to be at Hampden."

A New Team
is Born

WITH the Cup Final defeat, the first of the great Bolton Wanderers sides of the Fifties began to break up and the rebuilding process saw a new side emerge that was largely the product of the club's youth policy. Throughout the Fifties, the Wanderers played attractive football and were frequently competing for the championship without ever winning the ultimate prize.

Eddie Hopkinson explained: "The mid-Fifties were a transitional period. With the exception of Nat Lofthouse and Doug Holden, the bulk of the 1953 side started to drift away. They were mostly in their thirties now. Bolton had a wealth of good young players who were the product of the club's scouting system. We were one of the first clubs to try to catch them young rather than go out and buy, and they were spotting talented players down to schoolboy level. Because they arrived young, it meant there was a chance to give them a good grounding in Central League football before they moved up to the first team."

Players like Bryan Edwards and John Higgins would play key roles in the Wanderers side of the late Fifties. The signing of Edwards was typical of how Bolton operated and of the efficiency of the scouting network that had been established. He was recognised as a talent while playing in an under-16 league for Oulton Youth Club in his home city of Leeds. He first signed amateur forms, but as soon as he reached seventeen he had so impressed that he was offered a professional contract. National Service interrupted his career, but he established himself in the first team at the start of the 1954-55 season, at the expense of Eric Bell. A wing-half, he missed only one League game in the following three seasons and played in the 1958 Cup Final. Towards the end of his career he switched to the centre of defence and stayed with Bolton until April 1965. In all he played 518 League and Cup games for Bolton. He certainly represented a bargain which manager Bill Ridding would have appreciated for that £10 signing-on fee.

One player who did not have to serve too long an apprenticeship before breaking into the side, and remaining as first choice full-back for the rest of the decade, was Tommy Banks. After his mauling by Stanley Matthews in the 1953 Final, his elder brother Ralph had played his last game for Wanderers. Ralph had made his first appearance for the side in the opening Football League North fixture – a 2-1 win at home to Oldham – in January 1941, after the club had been closed for six months. Ralph's career had been severely interrupted by the war and then National Service. He was never a regular first choice after the 1948-49 season, but regained his place in time for the Final. Brother Tommy was one of his strongest competitors for the number-three jersey leading up to the Wembley game.

Tommy reveals that even with the departure of his brother, he still felt his future at Wanderers was limited because of the arrival of John Higgins, who was a similar age. Having been courted by Wolves before he signed for Bolton, Banks thought his future might be there, but the powers-that-be refused his transfer request. That he had no choice in the matter is something that still rankles.

Higgins was to have a glorious future at Wanderers, but not

as a full-back, even though that was his position when he arrived in 1950 from Buxton Town. His first senior outing was in a 1-0 win at Burnley in March 1953, at centre-half for the injured Malcolm Barrass. It was not until Barrass's departure to Sheffield United in 1956 that he made the first team regularly at centre-half and was first choice during the 1958 Cup-winning season. A far from worthy note in his career came in February 1960 when he became the first Wanderers player to be sent off since the war, in a game at Sheffield Wednesday. He retired from League football in 1961.

Florence Brandwood was, of course, still one of Bolton's ardent fans, but explains that the changes taking place at the club happened gradually and weren't really apparent to supporters at the time. "Looking back, you can see that the whole side changed within a couple of years, as the 1953 side got old and moved on, but at the time as a fan you didn't really notice. It is not as though they arrived one Saturday as a brand new eleven. They were new individuals and the crowd quickly took to them as they settled in. We were playing good football and it was a great time to be a fan. The post-war enthusiasm was still there and the cost of a day at the football was still cheap. We didn't have new players who grabbed the headlines, because there were no big transfer deals. Bill Ridding didn't go for big-name signings. I sometimes went to reserve team games and it was good to see some of the youngsters from that side starting to come into the first team and do so well. We had the makings of a good team and it was a good time to be a Wanderers supporter."

Their best season up until the Cup Final year of 1958 was the one immediately after their Wembley disappointment in 1953. In typical fashion there were some good home performances as Burnden Park again proved a difficult place for teams to visit. The away form, though, was the recurring problem. Four wins on their travels was not championship form although Wanderers finished the campaign in a respectable fifth place. In the Cup they reached the sixth round, only to lose a replay against Sheffield Wednesday at Burnden Park in a disappointing game best forgotten.

Certainly for Tom Hodgkinson, with his enthusiasm strengthened by the dramatic conclusion to the Cup Final, this was an ideal season to keep his interest. He became a regular at Burnden Park now and his new-found loyalty was rewarded with a season that had the terraces in full voice. "We had a good run in the League and Cup and there was a real buzz about the club and the supporters. Certainly there was no shortage of excitement. There was also the feeling that the old team was breaking up and exciting new players were coming into the side and capturing everybody's imagination. The team that would contest the 1958 Final was more my team. I had watched them come through into the first team and I was closer in age to them."

During the 1953-54 campaign, Burnden Park had been a fortress with five wins and three draws since the start of the season. Next up on November 7 were Portsmouth and they were to be on the receiving end of a six-goal blitz, reinforcing the strength of Wanderers as a home side and reinforcing their top-six place in the table. The visitors had won at Burnden Park convincingly in their previous two seasons, but that was to end. A goal within five minutes when a clearance by Stan Hanson was seized on by Lofthouse, who ran from just inside the Portsmouth half before shooting low past the opposing 'keeper, was a sign of things to come. There was a hat-trick for Hassall and a second for Lofthouse, with Holden also getting in on the act. Portsmouth's only goal came from a Harris penalty.

It was not until February 13 that Bolton's home fortunes ran out and it was a sublime performance by Tom Finney that was their undoing as he orchestrated a 2-0 win, scoring the second himself after dribbling through defenders until he had only the 'keeper Ken Grieves to beat and then firmly placed it out of his reach. Bolton's cause was not helped by illness and injury which saw three enforced changes. The most serious of these was the loss of Hanson in goal, the first game he had missed in two years, and even worse, the ankle injury which kept Lofthouse sidelined.

The crowd was large enough that they spilled on to the perimeter track and they were entertained by some skilful football from both sides despite the heavy ground. To the dismay of the home support, though, it soon became clear that Finney was inspiring Preston to higher levels. Bolton squandered a good chance when a ball from Wheeler was not cleared by a Preston defender and the ball fell to Ronnie Codd, the replacement for Lofthouse, who tried and failed to dribble round the 'keeper.

It proved a costly miss because with only four minutes of the half remaining, a Finney corner was only half cleared and Baxter gave the visitors the lead. As the game wore on, Preston wisely kept the ball out wide to avoid the worst of the mud in midfield, and Finney's final flourish was a just reward for his superb display against a team desperate for the final whistle.

With the League challenge faltering, the Bolton players were determined to get back to Wembley and avenge their last-gasp defeat at the hands of Blackpool. It would also be a chance to repay the supporters for their magnificent homecoming by this time bringing them something back to cheer. The early rounds went well with Liverpool being defeated thanks to a Willie Moir goal and then non-League Headington United were swept away 4-2. After a home draw with Portsmouth, the Scottish international Moir was again on target with his two goals ensuring a fourth-round tie against Sheffield Wednesday.

Bolton crossed the Pennines and did the hard work securing a draw that earned a replay at Burnden Park. The town was again gripped by Cup fever and a sense that perhaps they would get a second chance at the Twin Towers. They were to be disappointed, however, as the home side conceded two soft goals from breakaways against the run of play to limp out of the competition. Given it was a midweek fixture, a crowd of 52,000 was an amazing turnout and proof of how the Cup had excited passions in Bolton. As the fans trudged home, the general view was that this was a match to forget. Too many key players, including Moir and Stevens, had underperformed and the loss of Wheeler merely compounded the problem.

Brandwood recalls these early seasons after the 1953 Final, saying: "Each year we would think that this was the one where we would win the League championship. There would be some good wins and days when we played like champions, but we never seemed quite able to do it. I was going to all the home and away games and you have to take the good days with the bad. After the disappointment of missing out on the Cup in 1953, it would have been marvellous if we could have gone back the following year, but we played a really bad game at home to Sheffield Wednesday and that was it. You only get one chance in the Cup."

Wanderers started the 1954-55 season well with a good win over Charlton on a typical Burnden mudbath, thanks to heavy rain through the morning. Bolton had the better start and put the Charlton defence under pressure with good attacking moves, but it was the visitors who scored first from the only quality attacking move they had produced in the first twenty minutes. A good cross from the by-line saw Hanson and centre-half Barrass collide and Charlton profited. Hassall equalised when a poor clearance fell kindly at his feet, and two minutes later Webster had time and space to safely slot the ball home from eight yards. As the seconds ticked by to end the half, the visitors equalised. In the second half both teams tired and the quality of the play suffered, but a Lofthouse header ensured Bolton collected the points and enjoyed a morale-boosting start to the season.

Alas, it would ultimately be a disappointing year for the first team, although the home fans at least had the unexpected consolation of a thrashing of Wolverhampton Wanderers that flew in the face of the form book. Bolton had gone seven games without a win when a Parry hat-trick inspired them to a 6-1 victory, although at half-time only one goal had been scored. Lofthouse had guided an Edwards clearance to the feet of Parry who hit it on the half-volley.

Within a minute of the restart it was a repeat of the opener, only with Bell supplying the finish. Wolves pulled one back, but it was a temporary hiccup for Wanderers who conjured up an inspired performance to open the Wolves defence. It sparked a mini revival for the club who went on to win three of their next four games in what proved their most productive spell of the season. They still only managed eighteenth in the League though.

The season did, however, see success come to Burnden Park and it would be a triumph that gave a portent to the future. The club won the Central League with a reserve team packed with players who would soon graduate to the first team as the second great team of the decade came into being. Roy Hartle explained: "In those days the Central League was much more important and was keenly contested. Myself and players like Higgins and Edwards were among maybe seven of the 1958 team who were at that time playing in the Reserves. We were building the team spirit that was going to be so important in the future. This was a period when Wanderers were finding their way as they developed a new side."

Another season came and 1955-56 saw another workmanlike campaign for the Wanderers who finished eighth, seventeen points behind the eventual champions Manchester United. There were, though, some highlights, not least a glorious week in December when ten goals were scored in two home games without the visitors troubling the scoreboard. After Lofthouse collected four goals in a 6-0 drubbing of Birmingham City, the fans wanted more of the same when Chelsea were the visitors and they weren't disappointed. Lofthouse was again in irrepressible form, collecting a hat-trick. The first was a textbook header to convert a Parry cross. Chelsea had won the League the previous year, but didn't look like champions now as Ralph Gubbins extended the lead before half-time. Two second-half goals underlined Wanderers' supremacy. Another Lofthouse header, this time from a Holden cross, and then a solo effort revived hopes of a championship challenge. Sadly, the two wins merely flattered to deceive the home fans and four League defeats over the Christmas and New Year period ended any hopes. For the second successive season, Bolton limped out of the Cup in the fourth round. This time to a 2-1 home defeat by Sheffield United.

The 1956-57 season saw Eddie Hopkinson get his chance in the first team in somewhat unusual circumstances. The Wanderers regular first-choice 'keeper, Ken Grieves, also played county cricket for Lancashire and there was an agreement between Wanderers and the cricket club that if Bolton were challenging for honours at the end of the season, then the player's release would be delayed, but also if at the end of summer Lancashire were in the title hunt, then he would remain there. That year Lancashire were chasing the championship and so a vacancy arose at the start of the season. The following year was also his testimonial year for Lancashire and so Grieves never returned.

Even so, it was not certain that Hopkinson would get to fill the empty berth as he was third choice 'keeper behind both Grieves and a youngster called Joe Dean, who had played for England at schoolboy level. A practice game was arranged and his place in the also-rans meant he had to face Nat Lofthouse. The second string won and Hopkinson thought he had played quite well. He was right and the team on the dressing-room wall for the opening match of the season included his name.

"The trouble was we were playing Blackpool and Stanley Matthews, which was the last thing I wanted for my first game," he said. "I had dreams about Matthews dribbling down the wing, cutting back before sending over a cross. On the day it took him twenty minutes to do just that – and Blackpool scored. All the nightmares came flooding back. They were soon banished, though, because we went on to win 4-1 and I was never out of the side for fifteen years."

Hopkinson revealed he had been on the point of retiring from professional football, but his wife urged him to try for one more season to fulfil his ambition of playing first-team football for the Wanderers. Fate meant he got his chance and he made the most of it. "There are so many elements of luck in this game that make the difference between making it and not. The thing is when you get your chance, you have to make the most of it. Some people blow it – but happily I didn't."

At only five feet nine inches tall, Hopkinson would be dwarfed by today's 'keepers, and even in the Fifties he was one of the smallest goalkeepers in the First Division, but it was never a problem for a player who was capped fourteen times for England. "It never bothered me. I used to say that height didn't matter because when I had my hands in the air I was six feet nine and I would defy anybody to jump higher than that."

Hopkinson was famed for his incredible bravery at a time when 'keepers received far less protection than their modern counterparts. He remembers a notorious hard man defender being sent forward with the sole purpose of clattering him. Fortunately, although he chased Hopkinson around the penalty box, he was never quite able to catch up with the Bolton man. His injury list, though, shows he was not always so lucky in his exchanges with forwards. It includes 47 stitches, ten broken or dislocated fingers, a broken leg, septicaemia and a ruptured kidney. He considers it could have been a lot worse throughout a long career. And he adds that he has never pulled a muscle.

Among his team mates there was another trait Hopkinson was noted for. He never accepted the blame for a goal while he was on the field. He says he is not superstitious and didn't get nervous before the game, although he did afterwards, but it was important for him that there was always somebody else at fault for a goal. He believes it would have affected his confidence if he started taking responsibility for conceding goals. Bryan Edwards, for one, did not always agree, which sometimes sparked lively discussions on the field when the defender was reluctant to take the blame.

Along with the building of a new team during this period, May 1957 also saw the installation of new floodlights that were 160 feet tall and allowed later kick-offs and night games to become a regular part of the Wanderers' calendar. The claim was that the power for the new lights would be sufficient to provide street lighting all the way from Burnden Park to Blackpool's Bloomfield Road. Whatever the validity of the assertion, it certainly provided fans with a talking point and more than 21,000 turned out to see Scottish First Division leaders Heart of Midlothian play the inaugural game under lights. They witnessed a 1-1 draw, although such was the mist that none of the 21,058 spectators had a clear view of the game. This was considered to be the fault of the freak weather conditions rather than any deficiency in the lighting system, but it was an unfortunate start to floodlit games at Burnden Park none the less.

Wanderers would finish the 1956-57 League campaign in ninth place to maintain their consistency, although a home third-round defeat by Blackpool in the Cup, 3-2, was a major disappointment. The perennial problem of poor away form again came back to haunt the side who could manage only three wins away from home. Remarkably, one was at Manchester United who had won the League championship the previous year and would do so again. Bolton, though, were to do the double over them. A 2-0 win at Old Trafford on March 25 came thanks to a goal by Parry and a Bill Foulkes own-goal.

The game that caught the imagination of the fans, though, was earlier in the season when, on November 10, the Busby Babes visited Burnden and ensured a record home League attendance for the season of nearly 40,000. The opening exchanges belonged to United, but the first goal went to Bolton when Holden made a foray into the penalty box and collected a square pass before shooting inside the far post with the 'keeper being given no chance. The defences limited chances for both sides, but Bolton got the second to ensure a 2-0 win when Stevens found Allcock who placed a clever shot past goalkeeper Ray Wood as he came off his line. For the fans packed on the terraces, almost as popular as the goals were some crunching tackles on the United winger Johnny Berry by Banks.

A chance to underline that on their day, Bolton could put poor form behind them and produce some stunning football, came with the visit of Leeds United in January 1957. The game was just a week after the disappointing Cup defeat against Blackpool, but gave the fans something to cheer as Wanderers triumphed 5-3 with an astonishing five goals coming in the first 23 minutes.

Bolton drew first blood after four minutes when Webster set up Gubbins whose shot beat Wood in the Leeds goal. However, two goals by John Charles, the first when he charged through the centre of the park before beating Hopkinson with a powerful shot and the second when he headed home a Meek free-kick, gave the visitors the lead. Two Lofthouse goals ensured that lead had lasted only three minutes. In the first he cleverly deceived Marsden to find space for a run and shot, and for the second a close-range shot left Wood standing. Before half-time the lead was increased when Lofthouse challenged for a cross with two Leeds defenders and the full-back Dunn conceded an own-goal. As the game degenerated into a bad-tempered affair, Leeds reduced the deficit thanks to a Meek shot, but Bolton had the last word with Holden firing a shot from twenty yards into the net with five minutes remaining. As they had against Manchester United, Wanderers again showed they could beat the best in one-off games, but they lacked the consistency to maintain a championship challenge. It would, though, bode well for the following season's Cup run.

Nat Lofthouse

WITH characteristic modesty, Nat Lofthouse says of his ability as one of the greatest centre-forwards in English football: "I had three things I could do reasonably well; I could run, shoot and head." As all who saw him agree, he did those essentials far better than reasonably well. He was an icon of his age, famed for his exploits for both Wanderers and England.

In the Fifties he was also a centre-forward in the old tradition. He describes himself as a "battering-ram centre-forward." It is a description with which many a goalkeeper of the day would concur. The controversial incident in the 1958 Cup Final, in which the Manchester United goalkeeper Harry Gregg ended up in the back of the Wembley net along with the ball, was not the first of its kind. Many a First Division 'keeper was on the receiving end of a Lofthouse charge in the days when those minding the net were afforded little protection.

Indeed, apart from dark muttering among the "goalkeepers' union" – Lofthouse was one of many centre-forwards of his day who regarded the 'keeper as fair game – the only others who found it a problem were the statisticians. Should the goal be credited to the player whose shot forced the save? Or the charging shoulder of the centre-forward?

In his excellent book *Bolton Wanderers: A Complete Record* the club's statistician Simon Marland, while relating basic details of a bruising encounter with Sheffield United in 1957, which was won 3-2, adds the footnote: "Some records credit Lofthouse with two goals, the goal in question coming from a shot by Hennin that was caught by the goalkeeper only for Lofthouse to barge both player and ball over the line." The official record says it all.

The Wanderers 'keeper Eddie Hopkinson was never on the receiving end of a Lofthouse charge, but having seen him in action he has no hesitation in saying that he was a complete centre-forward: "He was untouchable and there are not many football legends that can stand comparison with him. He is still the greatest header of a ball I have seen and, despite being only five feet ten inches tall, was very strong in the air. He is a great guy and Bolton Wanderers mad. I think he cries when Bolton lose. He has given sixty years of service to the club, man and boy, and his name is synonymous with Bolton Wanderers."

Ian Greaves saw Lofthouse from a defenders' point of view and has little doubt about his talents or the fact that he would be a force in the modern game, although he finds such comparisons odious. He also believes that Lofthouse is being a little disingenuous in playing down his footballing skills, even if natural modesty is the reason. "If he pretends he was anything other than a very good player able to hold his own with any of his generation, then he is telling fibs," he said.

And Greaves adds: "The player he most reminds me of in the modern game is Alan Shearer. There is a lot of Nat in Shearer, in that they are both strong, robust players, good in the air and willing to work hard and hustle. Nat was a very good player and people who say he didn't have good ball skills miss the point. He scored goals and that is what the game is about. Any player with his record has to be fabulous."

Tommy Banks also has no doubts about Lofthouse's pivotal role in the side. "He was our key player. He had his off days – nobody can play at the top of their game all the time – but he didn't have too many. He was as strong as a horse. I think Alan Shearer is a second Nat Lofthouse, but if I was honest I'd say Nat was quicker. He was fast. He would have been worth a lot of money in the modern game."

However, Lofthouse played at a time when there were no fortunes to be made by football talent, although the two white five-pound notes he received as his signing-on fee represented a month's wages to his father. During his career there were also books he was involved in and other minor sources of additional revenue, but nothing like the commercial fortunes a modern player can generate through sponsorship and the like.

There were not even a few little perks perhaps denied to the man in the street, like first-class travel for example. He recalls travelling with Tom Finney to London for an England game at Wembley when they were both in third-class and had to stand all the way. It has, though, kept him down to earth. He was known in his playing days, and still is by all who meet him, as "Lofty" – a monicker that perhaps sounds overly familiar yet which is one he likes. Perhaps because it marks him out as one of the people, in touch with his Bolton roots, rather than someone whose footballing skills have led him to become distant and perhaps even arrogant.

"I like it because when people call me Lofty, it is a form of friendship," he said. "They feel they know me and the sort of person I am. Even players I meet nowadays call me Lofty. I like meeting people and talking about football and Bolton Wanderers." A little cameo, related by lifetime supporter Fred Guest, gives an insight into the generous and warm character that is Lofthouse. As a local businessman and keen Wanderers fan, Guest had met Lofthouse down the years and they had chatted football first when he was a player and then as club president. When he heard it was Guest's 80th birthday, he joined them for a chat after a Bolton game and after offering his congratulations he quietly passed a limited edition commemorative plate over, unseen by anybody and without any ostentation. It is a treasured memento that now hangs with pride in the Guest home.

Bert Gregory also remembers Lofthouse's self doubt in his early days. Once Lofthouse joined him for a cup of tea after training and admitted he didn't think he was a good footballer. Gregory reassured him that although he might not be a ball player, he scored goals and that was what mattered. Gregory adds that he never remembers seeing Lofthouse have a bad game. That might owe something to a hazy memory on the octogenarian's part, but it is a view that would certainly find favour with many fans who saw him play in his prime. As Gregory says: "He was hard to knock off the ball and he let defenders know he was there. He wasn't one to demonstrate or draw attention to himself if things didn't go his way. Off the field he was very friendly and a grand lad."

There is no doubting Lofthouse's roots. He was born and bred in Bolton. He still lives in the town and is respected by – but still at one with – the local community. He still occasionally pops down to his local for a pint. The youngest of four sons, he was born on August 27, 1925. His father worked for Bolton Corporation. Even as a schoolboy, his prowess as a centre-forward was evident, although his first experience of organised football was one to forget; his side conceded seven goals and he was the goalkeeper. It didn't take him long to swop goalsaving for goalscoring.

He was soon attracting the attention of his home town club and signed as a 14-year-old amateur in 1939. It was on March 22, 1941, when aged 15 years 207 days, that he made his first-team debut and led the attack against close neighbours Bury in a Football League North match. It was likely to be a fierce contest as the Wanderers were looking to avenge a 4-1 defeat a week earlier.

Early chances to open his account were missed, but as the second half progressed, Lofthouse settled and with the game already safely secure, he completed a successful debut by scoring the fourth and fifth goals. A 5-1 victory had settled the account nicely and ensured the youngster kept his place in the side for the remainder of the season. That he scored eleven goals in as many games showed the young centre-forward was already honing his prolific goalscoring skills.

Many of the regular first-teamers were away at war. Indeed, Bolton Wanderers were one of only two clubs – the other being West Ham – who signed up for war duty virtually en masse. Fifteen professionals from Bolton enlisted in May 1939 and when war was declared in the September, they were all called up. It meant for the younger professionals who arrived later that there were first-team opportunities in wartime games.

Lofthouse certainly did not shirk his wartime duties. He was one of many in the new-look squad – Tommy Banks, Malcolm Barrass and Harry Hubbick were others – who combined amateur and part-time football careers with working as coal miners. The hard work of pushing tubs of coal down the pit certainly hardened him physically. It was, though, gruelling having to end eight-hour night shifts before setting out for football matches. He described himself at this time as lean and hard as nails with not an ounce of fat on him.

After the war he quickly established himself as a regular in a side strengthened with the return of established professionals. Although there was tough competition among the centre-forwards of the day, by the end of the Forties he was already beginning to be talked of in terms of an international call up. In 1949 he scored four goals for an FA XI against the Army. And a year later he went on the FA's summer tour to Canada.

He won the first of his England caps against Yugoslavia at Highbury, scoring both goals in a 2-2 draw. Within a year he was established as first choice centre-forward for England, playing in eighteen matches in succession. It was one of those games that firmly established his place in the pantheon of all-time greats and earned him the sobriquet of "Lion of Vienna". Before a 65,000 crowd, in the Prater Stadium, Austria were to be the bit part players in his most famous performance.

Austria were regarded as one of the leading teams in Europe when England arrived for their match on May 25, 1952. Thousands of British soldiers based on the Rhine were in the stadium to cheer England on and with just eight minutes remaining, the match was tied two-apiece with Lofthouse and Jackie Sewell having scored. Austria were having the best of the play when Tom Finney hit a long pass through the middle, Lofthouse chased it for thirty yards and shot, colliding with the goalkeeper as he did so. It proved the winning goal, but Lofthouse did not see the ball enter the net, as he was knocked unconscious. He was carried off, but returned for the final minutes. His heroic performance led to him immediately being dubbed the Lion Of Vienna and he was later presented with a silver statuette of a lion clutching a football.

The occasion was reported in *The Times* thus: "For anybody who has ever seen or read football, Lofthouse will always be known as the Lion Of Vienna...It was his example all through the match that brought the scores of British soldiers pouring through the crowd at the end of the game to cheer him, lion-hearted, from the field."

That Finney provided the pass which led to the goal that changed his career is no surprise. The two played in England teams together on more than twenty occasions and on eighteen of them Finney laid on the goalscoring pass. Lofthouse describes him as the favourite player he appeared alongside. He adds that the Preston North End star was, with George Best, the most complete footballer he ever saw.

Lofthouse's international career appeared to be over after the 1955-56 season, despite having one of his best campaigns for Wanderers, scoring 32 goals in 36 games, with four in a 6-0 win over Birmingham City, and four international goals in five games. It meant he missed the chance to parade his skills in the 1958 World Cup.

He was, though, recalled later that year and equalled Tom

Finney's England goalscoring record. His last international was against Wales, also in 1958.

In 1953, Lofthouse was named as Footballer of the Year, shortly before he appeared in that year's Cup Final. It was an experience that left him elated, particularly as he won praise not just for his goalscoring, but also his conduct and sportsmanship as a player. Perhaps some in the modern era would care to dwell on such qualities, but as the player himself acknowledges, it is a different game now.

Indeed, comparisons between those days and the present are always tricky in all manner of ways. However, on two of the most common inquiries directed his way, Lofthouse has clear opinions. He is often asked whether the game is today cleaner or dirtier than it was in his heyday. Certainly he believes the niggling fouls and petulance were absent.

His view: "We had a lot of hard men playing in our day, but they weren't dirty. We had them on our side; players like Roy Hartle, Tommy Banks and John Higgins. Other sides had their hard players. Those guys in our side took no prisoners, but they were clean. They played for the ball hard."

The other question frequently asked is whether the players of the Fifties would have flourished in the modern game. "I don't think you can compare football of my era and today. There are too many variations in formations, tactics and players. I will say, though, that I think players like Stan Matthews and Tom Finney would be good players today."

When asked whether there would be a place for Lofthouse in today's game, the veil of modesty is again drawn down. Certainly he thinks modern defensive tactics make it more difficult to score goals and life for a centre-forward is much harder. He adds: "There would have been a place for me if I had Matthews and Finney on the wings. The simple truth is that no defender can stop the ball in the air except with his head. And if the ball was there, I could head it."

He cites the same two players as the reason for his England success. Again it is a modesty that fellow professionals believe hides the real strengths and determination of a player who excelled in an era when there were a lot of good centre-forwards around. He was direct, uncompromising and fearless. Goals were his business and he let nothing get in his way of scoring them.

He said: "I was lucky enough to have had Matthews and Finney on the wings in my England days, so why should I want to be clever with my feet? All we needed to do was give it to them two and they would get to the by-line and get the ball over, lace facing away, and I would have a good chance of getting to it with my head."

Although he played his entire career with Bolton, there were approaches for his services on three occasions he believes. The nature of the game then and the control the club had over players it was not always known, even by the player himself if a rival club was interested.

"I think the club was approached on three occasions, by Blackpool, Plymouth and Arsenal, although I'm not quite certain about Arsenal," he remembers. "Then there was an enquiry from a foreign team after the Austria game in 1952. I was tempted, but now I am really and truly glad that I didn't take up the offer. I couldn't have been any happier than I was at Bolton. It is as simple as that and it is the truth."

In the days of the maximum wage, he played for Bolton for fifteen seasons and at the height of his powers received a basic wage of £15. "I don't know of many players who have been at one club as long as me, but it was no big thing being at Bolton because they are such a good club you see. Of all the players who have played and left, I have never heard one call Bolton Wanderers so it must be a good club."

Gordon Taylor remembers the tremendous support Lofthouse gave the younger players. His boyhood hero had just retired from the game when Taylor arrived at Burnden Park, but he remembers playing alongside him in training. With Lofty in charge of the Reserves, the young players strived to do well for him. It represented a dream come true for the player who as a boy had been passed over the turnstiles to see a League game against Portsmouth in which Lofthouse scored. Afterwards the young Taylor waited in the tea room for the players and got Lofthouse's autograph. He still has the programme.

Florence Brandwood epitomises the fans' view when she says simply: "He was brilliant. He put Bolton on the map and even now he gets involved in the community. He presented the prizes at our darts league's annual meeting. He is very popular and a gentleman."

Lofthouse admits to still enjoying watching football, but when it is his beloved Wanderers playing – and it frequently is, given his role as president and ambassador for the club – he concedes it is difficult to be objective. After a sixty-year association with the club, feelings run deep.

He confessed: "If Bolton aren't playing I enjoy the game as a football match. But when it's Wanderers I get passionate when the match is on and I am biased. I can only see the eleven Bolton players on the field. I must admit sometimes it isn't enjoyable. In fact it can be bloody awful. I certainly don't watch it as a neutral spectator and I can understand why people jump up and get excited when watching their team."

The end to his illustrious playing career came on December 17, 1960, in a game against Birmingham, a 2-2 draw at St Andrew's. Injured during a tour to South Africa, he had already missed the previous season. Now this cruciate ligament injury effectively finished him, although there was a brief attempt at a comeback the following year, but it was impossible.

Lofthouse exited as a player, leaving behind an enviable record as well as many happy memories for those privileged to see him play. He won 33 full England caps, scoring what was then a record thirty goals. In 503 appearances for Wanderers in

League and Cup between 1945-46 and 1960-61, he netted 285 times.

After running a pub for a while, he returned to Burnden Park in another role. This time as manager. In August 1968, Bill Ridding departed and Lofthouse was appointed, first temporary manager, before finally taking on the role full-time. It didn't last long as he struggled with little money or success. In November 1970, Jimmy McIlroy was appointed manager. Lofthouse three times more stepped up in managerial appointments that were shortlived.

He later admitted that going into management was not a good move: "It was the worse thing that ever happened to me. I wasn't a good manager. I could have been a good number two, but I couldn't do it as the big cheese. You have to know your own mind and make the tough decisions and have a good staff around you. There is also the respect of the players to be won over. They may respect you as a player, but you need to earn respect as a manager. I just wasn't cut out for the job. I used to lie awake at night if I had to drop a bloke the next day."

His association with the club continues to this day, however, with his role as the club's president. He still has an office at the new Reebok Stadium on the outskirts of town and is there most days. It completes a lifetime of devotion to Bolton Wanderers and enables him to do what he likes best; talk about football and Bolton and act as an ambassador for the club he has served so well. His great ambition now is that Bolton can return to the top flight where he knows they belong. If they make it, nobody will be cheering louder in the stands than Lofty himself.

Back on the Wembley Trail

T HIS was to be the year that Bolton Wanderers returned to Wembley and made amends for the defeat they had suffered five years earlier at the hands of Blackpool. Yet the opening fixture in the FA Cup campaign of 1958 was as tough as they come. A visit to Tom Finney's Preston North End was always likely to be a severe test for the Wanderers, but it brought out the best in them and they produced one of the finest displays of the season to produce a comfortable 3-0 victory and overcome the first hurdle on the road to the Twin Towers.

A crowd of 32,641 were squeezed into Deepdale and home fans were confident of seeing their side to victory. Preston were in great form and would end the League championship season as runners-up. However, their Cup dreams were about to be shattered. After a goalless first half, three goals in fifteen minutes of the second period saw Bolton through. It was a fully deserved win with two goals for Ray Parry and one for Dennis Stevens.

Stevens was a cousin of the Busby Babe Duncan Edwards, who would soon perish along with Manchester United team mates in the Munich air disaster. Stevens had been signed by Bolton as a 15-year-old when he was spotted playing for Worcestershire

Boys. He signed professional forms in December 1950, but it wasn't until the retirement through injury of Harold Hassall in 1955 that he made the inside-forward position his own. He represented the Football League and won two under-23 England caps, but never represented England, although he was called into the senior squad in April 1957.

Eddie Hopkinson recalls before the Preston game: "When we saw the draw, there was a feeling that it couldn't have been any harder for the third round of the Cup. To go there when Tom Finney was at his prime and win 3-0 was a remarkable result. That performance set us on our way and gave us the confidence to believe we could go all the way."

Tommy Banks also approached the tie with some trepidation. In a modern world of physically big players, he has no doubt that there would still have been a place for the maestro Tom Finney. Words fail him when he comes to describe the talent of the North End star. And he admits that he rarely had a good game against the player who could seemingly mesmerise defenders at will. "I never played Tom Finney well and it was a godsend to me that day that they played him on the left and Roy Hartle stopped him. By the time they switched wings in the second half, Roy had taken the edge off him. That was a good win and it had been a hard start for us."

Florence Brandwood was again at the ground bright and early to ensure she got right to the front so that her son David, then just three, could see some of the action. Bolton manager Bill Ridding saw the youngster and, ruffling his hair, said: "This must be our youngest supporter. Has he come to bring us luck?" Brandwood says: "I don't know about David bringing luck, but it was certainly a brilliant Wanderers performance. Although it was early days the fans were already thinking about Wembley. As a supporter you always live in hope, but it was a great day. Preston were always a good team in those days. But we had a great Cup tradition and we always felt we could do well, even though the previous few seasons had been disappointing. This time we hoped things would go right, but you always need a bit of luck as well in the Cup."

Bolton were on the road again for the fourth round and this time visited York, where the home side rode their luck in a game played on an atrocious pitch. Wanderers never looked like losing, but were unable to convert their attacking prowess into goals. The nearest they came was in the second half when Lofthouse put the ball in the net, but the goal was ruled out for offside. Banks recalls "There was ice under the ground and because it had been raining, the pitch was waterlogged. They were the luckiest team in the world to get a draw and we should have decided it there." York had earned a replay, but Bolton were not going to let them off the hook again and 3-0 was a comfortable victory for the home side.

Crowd trouble is something more associated with the modern game, at least from the Seventies onwards, but Brandwood remembers the York match because she ended up in hospital after a rival woman fan hit her with the rattles so common at football matches then. Nowadays they would probably be regarded as dangerous weapons and banned. Certainly Brandwood can testify that in the wrong hands they can deliver a mean blow.

She explained she had been in the stand and turned to say hello to Nat Lofthouse's wife when the woman next to her accused the Bolton star of being a dirty player. Brandwood leapt to the defence of her team's star player and got clocked with the rattle for her trouble. She came round with St John's Ambulance volunteers bandaging her head.

It was the York replay that led to the threat of the sack for anybody at the mill where she worked who went missing for the afternoon. Brandwood promptly did. As she says, she wasn't going to miss a Wanderers Cup-tie. She didn't even bother going in for work the next day. A van called round to say she was needed – partly because the mill was short staffed, but also because she had promised to get the boss a ticket for the Final if she possibly could and if Wanderers managed to get there. The feeling in the town was that this would be their year.

Stoke City were the visitors in the next round and more than 56,000 fans braved driving rain to see the game. They were nearly disappointed as it needed a last-minute pitch inspection by the referee before he finally gave the go-ahead for the match to be played. It meant typical Wanderers conditions of a heavy, muddy pitch liberally littered with puddles and the home side duly thrived. Hopkinson admits that the game wouldn't have been played nowadays, with puddles the size of cricket pitches and horrendous conditions.

The opening goal saw Stevens collect a Hennin clearance and slip the ball to Lofthouse who scored with a well-hit shot. After the break it was Stevens himself who got on the scoresheet with a half-volley shot from a Birch cross. The home side were dominating and another goal seemed inevitable. It came from Parry, with a reflex goal that saw him react the quickest when the ball hit the bar. A goal for Cairns with only six minutes remaining was little consolation for the Stoke fans who had endured the rain to witness the battle of the Burnden mud.

Wolverhampton Wanderers arrived at Burnden with hopes of a League and Cup double still intact. They were to comfortably clinch the League title, but their Cup hopes were ended in a thrilling encounter before a crowd of just over 56,000. Again there had been worries about the state of the pitch, but it was in good condition on the day. Wolves had the best of the play and at times threatened to overwhelm the home side in the first meeting of the clubs in the Cup for 56 years. However, Bolton battled hard and made the most of the lucky breaks that came their way. Stevens collected the opener against the run of play after 25 minutes when Lofthouse fed Birch, who raced away and crossed before Wolves defenders had time to regroup; Stevens sidefooted into the net. Wolves quickly equalised to leave the sores level at half-time. The winner came after a linesman spotted the Wolves 'keeper carrying the ball outside his area and awarded a free-kick from around thirty yards out. Under siege at the back, it was a rare respite for the Bolton defenders and Banks remembers coming up for the kick and urging Ray Parry to have a shot. "He hit the ball like a rocket and in it went. It was after this game I said to everyone, if we can win this game we can win the Cup. It gave us a lot of confidence."

Hopkinson describes the game as "like the Alamo" as the Bolton defence withstood wave after wave of Wolves attacks as the visitors pushed men forward and kept pumping the ball into the penalty box in search of the goal they desperately needed. It was a continuous battle in which the 'keeper excelled, saving shot after shot. Such was the intensity of the match at one point that Parry went off with exhaustion. And there were no subs in those days.

Lofthouse repeats the old football cliché that the side were taking each game as it came, but now years on he admits that it was after this match that for the first time he started to sense that this could be Bolton's year. "You need a bit of luck to get to Wembley and we certainly had it in that game. Wolves murdered us for three-quarters of the game and we struggled but we hung on for a narrow victory."

So to the semi-final and it was back to Maine Road, where the club triumphed on their way to the 1953 Final. This time Blackburn Rovers were the opponents and it proved a tough struggle. It was Rovers who took the lead from a corner-kick met by the head of Peter Dobing who steered the ball just inside the post. Blackburn had two more great chances and were to regret not taking them as Bolton hit back.

Lofthouse was injured for the game and that was certainly a worry for Tom Hodgkinson, although he felt that Ralph Gubbins was a fair player. "Lofthouse was the bees knees. I remembered him from the early days, but as I became more keen on

Wanderers, he was the player still there and he was the one we relied on. He bridged the gap between the two teams of the decade. To have reached the semi and got within a match of Wembley, for him to be injured was a blow for the fans."

He need not have worried as this was to be the stage for his replacement Ralph Gubbins to step out of the shadows and make his name. He signed for Bolton in 1952, after completing his military service, and started out playing inside-left. However, he moved out to the left wing and had the occasional runout as a centre-forward when the great Lofthouse was injured. He was to spend seven years at the club, but the semi-final was his finest hour.

He hit two goals in as many minutes to earn himself a place in Wanderers folklore and his side a trip to Wembley. A pass into the penalty area beat defenders who were all claiming offside. Gubbins collected it and then dribbled round the 'keeper to score his first. The crowd were still cheering that effort when, thanks to the swirling wind, a Banks free-kick deceived the 'keeper and fell to the feet of Lofthouse's very able replacement who made no mistake. The second half was a scrappy affair but there was relief for Bolton as the clock ticked down when a goal by Dobing was ruled out for offside.

Florence Guest remembers there was again the excitement and tension of the Cup and with only a one-goal lead there was never a chance for the fans to relax. It was just as it had been in the 1953 semi-final. "After the thrill of Gubbins scoring two goals in quick succession, everybody just wanted the game over. I feared they would get an equaliser and remembered how Everton had come back from much further behind in 1953. It is hard to describe the euphoria which success in the Cup brought to the town. After the disappointment of five years before we were convinced it would be our turn to celebrate."

For Hodgkinson the game went in a blur, although he can remember queuing two miles up Manchester Road to secure a

Sunday Pictorial

March 10, 1946.

No. 1,617

TWOPENCE

EILEEN

Her Story—on Page 5

The Most Horrible Game Ever Played

33 KILLED AT A CUP TIE—AND THEY WENT ON PLAYING FOOTBALL

The Twisted Bits Of Iron Caused It

The conscience of the nation will be shocked this morning by the news that while 33 people lay dead, mangled and suffocated and 500 injured were being treated, the Bolton v. Stoke Cup-Tie game yesterday continued to its end as though nothing had happened.

500 WERE INJURED

These few bent pieces of steel bars tell the story of the disaster. They are the remains of one of the two crush-bars that broke as the crowd surged in a pile of screaming humanity. The bars were forced out of their concrete bed by the stampede.

REFEREE of the match and the man who gave the decision to play on was Mr. G. Dutton, of Warwick, and he explained that he was advised to continue the game by the police.

"After the barrier broke, a police officer asked me if I would get the players into the dressing room until some order could be restored." he said.

"The police officer told me some people were dead, but I did not tell the teams. I called the two captains and told them to get the players into the dressing room. When order had been restored on the field, I gave the players' instructions to resume."

The players did not know the extent of the disaster.

F. Steele, the Stoke centre-forward, said: "Mr. Dutton came into the dressing-room and told the players, 'I have been asked by the Chief Constable of Bolton to request you to carry on with the game.' That was the first we knew.

"When we were going on the field, Baker, the outside left, and Pettit, inside right, were stopped by a man, who got hold of them and said: 'It is a crime for you to carry on with the match.'"

Nor did thousands of the onlookers know of the extent of the disaster. When play was resumed there was all the usual cheering and excitement of a Cup-tie.

WHAT WE THINK—P. 4

THIRTY-THREE spectators, one of them a woman, at the Bolton Wanderers football ground, were trampled to death or suffocated and 500 injured when two crush barriers collapsed under a seething weight and sent thousands surging downward in a terrible, irresistible wave of fighting and struggling humanity.

The disaster was caused by thousands of gate-crashers, who broke through the outside fences and forced the crowd, already a record of nearly 70,000, helplessly forward.

A quarter of an hour after the start of the game the jammed crowd began to sway bodily towards the pitch.

A waist-high crush wall, built to keep crowds back, collapsed under the tremendous weight and hundreds were shot down a slope, to be trampled on by the oncoming mass. On and on went the chaotic rush, and finally two iron crush barriers bent and cracked.

People tumbled and fell to death and injury knowing that they were trampling on other human beings and could not avoid it. Those at the front were swept in their hundreds on to the pitch.

The referee stopped the game and the players pushed their way to the dressing-rooms, but after 26 minutes, on police advice after the pitch had been cleared by mounted men, play was resumed.

The players had little idea of the extent of the tragedy. Nor had half the people in the ground, and they roared and cheered the game.

And all the time dead bodies were being pulled out from helpless piles of half-conscious injured people. The dead were carried away to the mortuary, scores of severely crushed people were taken to hospital, and hundreds were treated where they lay.

Last night Bolton women besieged the mortuary, terrified lest they should recognise their missing menfolk, and there was a vast, tearful crowd outside the infirmary.

THE WHOLE STORY IS TOLD IN FULL ON THE BACK PAGE.

Why?

THE people of Bolton who were outside the ground were unaware of what had happened until the match was over.

Then, as they saw the crowd streaming away from the match they refused to believe rumours that a disaster had occurred in the middle of the game.

When the facts were confirmed and the news began to spread, Bolton was amazed and shocked.

The vicar of the town, Canon W. J. H. Davidson, told the "Sunday Pictorial": "Although I do not know all the circumstances, I am appalled that the game should have gone on afterwards.

"I should like to know why, and unless there was a very good reason, I can only condemn such a decision.

"The human thing to have done would have been to stop the game and send the people home."

"The conscience of the nation will be shocked…" How one national newspaper reported the Burnden tragedy of March 1946.

Bolton Wanderers team pictured in 1946-47. Back row (left to right): Gillies, Hamlett, Hanson, Bill Ridding (trainer), Hubbick, Forrest. Front row: Woodward, Howe, Atkinson, Lofthouse, Westwood, Rothwell.

Bolton Wanderers team, 1948-49. Back row (left to right): Bill Ridding (trainer), Howe, Roberts, Hanson, R. Banks, Barrass, Murphy. Front row: Woodward, Moir, Lofthouse, Walter Rowley (manager), Bradley, McShane, Gillies.

Aston Villa's Tommy Thompson is challenged by John Higgins and Bryan Edwards of Bolton in the 1-1 draw at Villa Park in December 1951.

The Banks brothers, Tommy (left) and Ralph, pictured in October 1950.

Willie Moir (8) scores Bolton's second goal in the 1953 FA Cup Final.

Moir's joy was short-lived and at the end of the so-called 'Matthews Final' he congratulates the legendary Blackpool and England winger.

Bolton Wanderers team, 1953-54. Back row (left to right): Bill Ridding (manager), McIlwain, Wheeler, Ball, Hanson, Barrass, Bell, Lofthouse, Bert Sproston (trainer). Front: Codd, Holden, Moir, W. Hayward (chairman), Hassall, Higgins, Parry.

Doug Holden won five England caps. His Wanderers career saw him score 44 goals in 463 appearances from 1951-52 to 1962-63. He gained an FA Cup winners' medal in 1958.

'The Lion of Vienna' – Nat Lofthouse scored 285 goals in 503 League and Cup appearances for Bolton in a career which spanned 1945-46 to 1960-61, as well as setting a new record for England goals.

Dennis Stevens was another member of the 1958 FA Cup-winning side and, in 1959-60, finished as Bolton's leading League scorer after taking over from the injured Nat Lofthouse. In all he scored 101 goals in 310 appearances.

Ray Parry was a member of a famous Derby footballing family but he chose Bolton and went on to make two appearances for England as well as 299 for Wanderers, scoring 79 goals . He was in the side which won the FA Cup in 1958.

Roy Hartle was unlucky to miss out in the 1953 FA Cup Final after playing in all the earlier rounds, but he captained the side which won the Cup in 1958. Altogether he made 499 appearances for Bolton, only one of them as a sub, and scored 13 goals.

Eddie Hopkinson made his Wanderers debut in 1956-57 after earlier slipping through Oldham Athletic's fingers. A member of the 1958 Cup-winning side, he made 578 senior appearances for Bolton and won 14 England caps.

Nat Lofthouse is jubilant after scoring Bolton's first goal in the first few minutes of the 1958 FA Cup Final against

Manchester United.

Manchester United goalkeeper Harry Gregg and the ball lie in the United net after the second Bolton goal when Lofthouse legitimately bundled Gregg over the line.

Nat Lofthouse is congratulated by fans after being presented with the FA Cup.

Eddie Hopkinson pictured with his children Karen and Paul and Snowy, the family's pet rabbit.

Dennis Stevens slots the ball home past Everton's Albert Dunlop at Burnden Park in August 1959. Bolton won 2-1.

Fans offer their autograph books to Hartle, Higgins and Lofthouse as they pound the track around Burnden Park in August 1960.

What a mesh! Hill, Hopkinson, Lofthouse and Higgins behind the wire at Burnden Park in August 1960.

Dennis Stevens receives treatment after being accidentally kicked in the face by Fulham's Roy Bentley (5) at Burnden Park in October 1960. Wanderers went down 3-0.

A 'Burnden Ballet' against Manchester City in November 1960 as Nat Lofthouse (on ground) comes a cropper against Bert Trautmann. Wanderers won 3-1.

In the game against Manchester City in November 1960, 16-year-old amateur Francis Lee made his League debut after only eight reserve matches, scored a goal and got himself booked. It was the start of a distinguished career in which he scored 106 goals in 210 senior games for Bolton and won 27 England caps.

Freddie Hill was another talent as Bolton's senior team continued to blood youngsters. In March 1963, as a member of the youngest forward line ever fielded by Bolton, Hill scored a hat-trick in a 3-2 Wanderers win over Sheffield United. He was later capped for England and altogether scored 79 goals in 412 senior appearances for Bolton.

Gordon Taylor worshipped Bolton Wanderers as a schoolboy. He went on to play for them 286 times, scoring 46 goals. Taylor is now one of the most influential men in the game as chief executive of the Professional Footballers' Association.

Doug Holden (partly hidden) wheels away after scoring against Blackburn Rovers at Ewood Park in April 1962. Dennis Butler joins in the celebrations but Blackburn's Keith Newton and Mike England look aghast. Bolton won 3-2.

Bill Russell scores in the 2-0 home win over Leicester City in May 1963. For Bolton, the season had been a struggle against relegation.

Bolton Wanderers' first-team squad pictured in August 1963. By the end of the season the Wanderers had lost their place in football's top division. They needed to beat Wolves in their last game but slumped 4-0 to end a 29-year period in the First Division.

ticket for the game. As he says, there was no such thing as buying off the internet or through specialist sports ticket agencies. He arrived at 5am to join the thousand or so already there before him and six hours were to pass before he collected the all-important ticket that would ensure him a place at Maine Road. He recalls that those waiting patiently did so with good humour and there was much banter.

Brandwood was again back on the pavement outside Burnden Park near the front of the queue to be sure of her ticket for the semi-final. She thought being back at Maine Road was a good omen because the 1953 semi against Everton was played there. "When we went behind, I still thought we would do it and then Ralph Gubbins got two goals in as many minutes and we just couldn't believe it. We were still cheering the first and then the second went in. I can't even remember the second goal. All I know is that everyone was so excited that the game couldn't be restarted immediately. I was among the crowd who spilled on to the edge of the pitch and I just stood there with my scarf, cheering for the team. A policeman told me to get off the pitch and the crowd started booing him for being a spoilsport. Lofty's face when we had won was a picture. I think he wanted to pick Gubbins up, but he had injured his shoulder. Before the game a few of the fans had feared the worst because Lofty was missing, but I had faith in Gubbins. You have to believe in all the players if you're a supporter or else it wouldn't be worth going."

Afterwards she waited along with hundreds of other ecstatic Bolton fans for all the players to come out of the dressing-room. Then she made her way to the long line of coaches that had ferried the faithful to Manchester. Everybody was singing on the way back. Another trip to Wembley and this time she believed the result would be different from 1953.

It is also a game of which Hopkinson in the Bolton goal has only vague memories after a clash with a Blackburn player in a classic one-to-one situation. "I went down against Ally McLeod and got caught by his foot and broke my cheekbone. I spent the last twenty minutes of the game in agony and seeing three balls. I just went for the middle one and it seemed to work. Bert Sproston, our trainer, spent the remainder of the game behind the goals talking to me and keeping an eye out for how I was. I suppose we had a bit of luck then, but all sides need that."

After a marathon encounter with Fulham that went to a replay, Manchester United had finally won through with the remains of a squad decimated by the Munich air disaster on February 6. Bolton now knew their opponents in the Final and how emotive an occasion the trip to Wembley was bound to be.

Tommy Banks believes the ramifications of the disaster affected English football and him personally in ways beyond the sheer horror of a tragedy that robbed the world of fine footballers. He is honest enough to admit that he would probably have never worn the England shirt but for the crash. The England full-back was Manchester United's Roger Byrne, who many believe was the first of the modern full-backs in the way he played. Byrne did not survive the air crash. "I know I was lucky to get in the England team. I think I would have been in the party, but as the reserve full-back," says Banks.

The Bolton player also believes that without the disaster which robbed the country of so many leading internationals, then England would have won the World Cup in Sweden in 1958. "I have always said we would have won the World Cup. I am convinced of it. That year we held Brazil to a goalless draw with a scratch team. With the Manchester United players who were lost, the World Cup would have been ours eight years earlier than it was and Manchester United would have been European champions in 1958. That's how much English football was set back."

Brandwood recalls that when it was known Manchester United were the opponents, the Bolton fans had to try to put all memories of the Munich crash out of their minds. When the news of the disaster broke, she had been working at the mill and was paid on piecework. The more work you did, the more money you got. She earned virtually nothing that day as workers gathered in small groups to discuss the disaster and pass on the latest news of the survivors. Now, though, the Bolton fans had to harden their hearts.

She explained: "We knew everybody would want United to win, but how often do you get to Wembley? We just had to shut our ears to all the talk of United and how they deserved to win the Cup. We were going down there to win. I'd been once before and knew what it was like to lose and I didn't want that feeling again. I'm sure the players thought the same."

The Post-
Munich Final

THE 1958 FA Cup Final was the 30th played at Wembley and one of the most emotive and controversial although it is fair to say not the most artistic. It pitted Bolton, who had not bought a player in eight years, against Manchester United, struggling to create a new generation of Busby Babes after the horrors of the Munich air disaster.

The old clash in approach was still there. Bolton were deemed workmanlike, an echo of the Malcolm Barrass verdict in the Forties and still applicable a decade on. There were no claims to glamour and their only star was Nat Lofthouse, although there were question-marks over how well he had recovered from the shoulder injury that kept him out of the semi-final. They were considered a strong defensive side, but also capable of producing brilliant attacking moves at times.

Meanwhile, as they had in the years before, and would continue to do until this day, United were the team that trawled the country looking to find players, and for them money was no object. There was also a sense that many of the young players being given their chance were talented and would have made the first teams at other clubs probably far sooner, also an echo of the squad system at Old Trafford today.

Ian Greaves had been on the fringes of the United first team and it was the Munich disaster that saw him gain a regular place and a chance to play at Wembley. The player himself, though, was just happy to be alive. As Manchester United had prepared to fly out for their tragic European Cup-tie, he had been playing for the Reserves. "I had been told to bring my kit and travelling bag with me because I was expecting to go as a replacement," he recalls. "In the bath after the match, the assistant trainer Jimmy Murphy came in and told me I wasn't going. They were taking my best mate Geoff Bent as cover for Roger Byrne, who was carrying an injury. Geoff never came back. I now celebrate two birthdays every year. One is on the day of the crash on February 6 because, but for the Grace of God, it would have been me there. I give a thought to the lads each year."

The fervour with which the nation willed the success of United was captured in a hyperbole-strewn front-page editorial in the *Manchester Evening News* on the eve of the Final that said: "Manchester United's Red Devils have won through to Wembley again ...it takes your breath away, it defies reason, it thrills, and it makes you both proud and humble. This is the most wondrous thing in the history of football, an epic story fired by death and the will to live. The Red Devils have not merely survived, they have added yet another chapter of success and the club is gloriously alive again."

Such outpourings of support left the Bolton players in no doubt that, their 15,000 supporters in the ground aside, the Wembley crowd and the nation were urging a United win and a fairytale finish for them in such a heartbreaking season. Memories of Stanley Matthews and the 1953 Final came flooding back. But Lofthouse had another memory. He recalls that after the 1953 Final the Blackpool captain Harry Johnston went into the Bolton dressing-room to pay his respects. "What are you doing here, Harry Johnston?" a voice called out. "If I were you at this moment I would be outside walking on top of the stands!" The words were spoken by Lofthouse and now five years later he hoped it would be his turn to, metaphorically speaking, walk on top of the Wembley stands.

There was another old face from the Blackpool game who was back to face them. Ernie Taylor, who Malcolm Barrass had highlighted as a key figure in Bolton's late demise with his accurate passing finally unleashing Matthews, would now be providing the same service for Dennis Viollet and Bobby Charlton. The England international was now 32 and had been United's first signing after the disaster as the club looked to strengthen their playing squad.

Manchester United also had history on their side, although in their case it had been compromised by the Munich air crash. On all four previous occasions when the defeated Finalists had gone back to Wembley on the first attempt, they had gone home with the trophy. Experience of the Wembley atmosphere was seen as giving the team the edge, but in United's case six of the previous year's team had been killed and three seriously injured.

Greaves recalls it was a new team in many ways with some players recently acquired and others who hadn't really played first-team football. He had played twenty first-team games and that marked him down as almost a veteran. However, as the team battled through the FA Cup rounds, a spirit had begun to develop and by the Final, a real camaraderie had been forged.

"Good players can get you to the top but so too can team spirit and we started to feel we could play a bit. Perhaps we didn't know what we were doing properly, but we had gelled into an outfit that was already proving hard to beat, although we were certainly not the most talented team United have had," he said.

Eddie Hopkinson remembers the excitement during the build-up to the match. "If you ask any player what they would like to do in football, then to a man they will say to play in an FA Cup Final at Wembley. I think it is the pinnacle of everybody's career and here we were on the verge of achieving it. Up to the Final, the ambition is just to get there, but once you know it's the Final, then all that matters is winning. Nobody remembers the losers. Sport is all about winning."

Tommy Banks said that the team followed the same routine they had in 1953, even staying at the same hotel in Hendon. They also had a song that had been their Cup song since the early rounds. Coach George Taylor was a keen singer and was a member of a choir. He also liked walking and knew many of the songs from his youth hostel days. An old tune called *Abe My Boy* would still be being sung, although badly, as the celebrations carried on into the night, but that was for later.

The full-back remembers there was a confidence in the side and everybody was relaxed. While Bolton were up against the will of the nation, on the field the Manchester United side were now tragically a shadow of the team that had beaten them 7-2 in a League game only three months before. Banks recalls: "I was never as confident of winning a game as I was then. If I had been a betting man, I would have had money on us. Everybody was against us, as they were in 1953, but on the field there are still only eleven players facing you. To be honest I think we would have had a good game even if it was their full team."

And he believes Manchester United were better than a lot of people had given them credit for. There were some good young players and a few unsung heroes like Dennis Viollet, who Banks rates highly as a player. Bolton knew it was not going to be easy, but Banks remembers that the Wanderers had often had good results against United, whether it was the team of the Forties or the pre-Munich side of the Fifties.

There was some light training for the Bolton players in the days before the game, but nothing too strenuous. Tactics never played a huge part, but the general feeling was that the weak links for Manchester United were Ian Greaves and former Villa wing-half Stan Crowther and it would be up to the Bolton players Brian Birch and Dennis Stevens to exploit this weakness down

United's left flank. Defence was a traditional strong point for Wanderers and they were confident that Dennis Viollet and Bobby Charlton could be held in check.

While the Bolton players relaxed as best they could and waited for the big day, for some of their fans there was much to do. For some, the build-up to the game had brought huge disappointment before a ball was even kicked. Tom Hodgkinson had failed to get a ticket, despite being a regular fan, and even now he smarts at the way the tickets were distributed by Bolton. While United operated a token system which ensured that if a supporter had the required number of vouchers then a ticket was guaranteed, at Bolton the system was a first-come-first-served reliance on postal applications.

He said: "I never got a ticket, while people who never went to a match were getting them. How the system worked I don't know, but it meant I had to watch one of Bolton's greatest successes at home on television. You can't believe how disappointed I was to miss out."

Florence Brandwood had also received a brown envelope containing her postal orders. Her application for tickets had been unsuccessful and she was in danger of missing Bolton Wanderers big day out. She is also critical of the way tickets for the match were distributed. People who had never been regular supporters were able to get tickets because of their connections with directors or leading players, while genuine fans were now being left out. It is a complaint not confined to Bolton and certainly not one that blighted just the Fifties. Investigations into how touts and those in the corporate hospitality business get Cup Final tickets, and which individuals sold them, are as common today as they were then.

However, Brandwood was not to be denied her trip to the Twin Towers. She made her way to Burnden Park and asked to see the manager, Bill Ridding. "They asked me what I wanted to see him for, but I was not going to tell them I was after tickets. I knew the tickets were like gold dust and I'd never asked before. This was desperation. They took me to his office and I couldn't believe I was so far inside the stadium. None of the fans were allowed in there. I told him why I was there and he remembered me from the local newspaper because I had queued all night for the semi-final tickets. He gave me three for the Final. He wouldn't take any money for them either. I wanted to give him £1, but one of the staff there said he would be upset if I offered him money. I kept my hand on my pocket all the way home. I didn't dare take the tickets out to look at them because I was frightened of somebody snatching them."

On the day of the match she caught a coach leaving Bolton at midnight which arrived in London at 6am. Then she made her way straight to Wembley, even though it would be hours before the gates were open. She waited outside and saw the crowds grow from a trickle of fans to a dense mass of bodies. The time passed quickly, she explained, as there were quite a few people waiting and they talked football and were so excited they didn't notice the time. It meant she had the prime spot she wanted right at the front near the tunnel.

For Roy Hartle it was the highlight of his career and he remembers being terrified as the players made their way from the dressing-room. "I remember being in the tunnel and everybody is trying to kid on that there isn't a problem and they are quite relaxed. It is fairly quiet and you can hardly hear any noise from the crowd down there. Then suddenly the guys ahead start moving and you are walking up the tunnel and you get to the top and it is as though somebody has just lifted the lid off the place and the noise is incredible. What I remember most is that noise as you come up the tunnel. It was like hitting a wall of sound. There were 100,000 people in those days."

Greaves remembers it was three days before the events of the day fully sank in. He can recall walking out with the teams and the shivers were running down his spine. "There is something wonderful about Wembley. Even now, in places like Italy and Germany, the players there still think it is the place. It's always held that thrill. As I walked out I thought we could do it. We had got this far and we had the mental determination to go on."

The game itself was a dour affair, decided by two Lofthouse goals. His second was the infamous barge on United 'keeper Harry Gregg that will forever be shrouded in controversy. Nowadays the centre-forward would have been lucky to escape with a yellow rather than a red card. Over forty years ago, the goal stood. But Lofthouse himself now admits: "It was a very emotive game and the question I am always asked after Gregg was bundled into the net is, was it a foul or not? Yes it was. I have always been glad that we won by two goals. I see Harry quite often and he doesn't bother about it because he is a hell of a guy. When you consider this was a guy who went back into the aircraft to try to rescue some of his team mates, that is a measure of the man."

Gordon Taylor, watching the game on television, was a committed Bolton fan so while everybody else's sympathy was with Manchester United he was rooting for the Wanderers and with the myopia that comes only with being a passionate supporter, he saw nothing wrong with Lofthouse's second goal. "Of course, I felt it was a fair challenge. It was Gregg's own fault for trying to hold the ball while turning his back on the line. In those days shoulder-charges were all part of the game."

Hodgkinson takes a different view, saying he thought at the time it was a foul, but pointing out that Bolton were well on top anyway and would have been deserving winners without the controversy of the second Lofthouse goal. And the fans were thrilled that after the disappointment of the Blackpool Final, they had come back to win the Cup.

Banks jokes that when he sees Harry Gregg, he always tells him: "Thou were swanking, knocking it up saying 'it's mine.'

People, though, talk about that goal, but to be honest they never looked like scoring apart from a Bobby Charlton shot that hit the post. It was unfortunate and I'm not saying they wouldn't have won if it had been disallowed. You can't say that. But on the day we deserved it and I think we always had a bit of a downer on United. We always played well against them."

Seeing Harry Gregg flattened in that way, was all too much for Florence Guest, who had followed Bolton's Cup run with interest and was now in the stand as she had been in 1953. Having missed lunch, and with temperatures soaring on the hot, sunny day, the injury was the last straw and she fainted. She was carried to the edge of the tunnel, feeling so awful she says she didn't care who had scored. By the time of Bolton's homecoming, though, she was more than ready to celebrate their first Cup win since 1929.

Certainly, the row over the goal should not detract from a performance by Bolton that was superior all round. Hartle believes that it wasn't a good game and that Bolton should have scored more than two against a depleted Manchester United. "We should have gone on and really won it. I suppose we were satisfied."

Lofthouse's opener came as early as the third minute when he met a long, sweeping ball from left-half Edwards. On a glorious day, United were given little chance to shine and their attacking efforts were minimal. Their best chance fell to Charlton in the 54th minute, whose fierce shot hit a post and rebounded into Hopkinson's grateful hands. Three minutes later, a Stevens shot was pushed into the air by Gregg. Lofthouse powered in, 'keeper and ball were in the net - and the game was effectively over.

Greaves thought he had played well enough and afterwards, because United had the sympathy vote, there was no real criticism of the players. He remembers going up for his medal and forgetting the last instruction to take his chewing gum out, so he went to the Royal Box chewing away. He is full of praise for the Bolton side and adds that nothing can be taken away from their performance.

Brandwood remembers saying, "Bad luck," to a United player after the game and in his despair he kicked the match ball high into the stand. Lofthouse had wanted the ball as a souvenir of his two-goal Cup performance, but it wasn't returned. Later he appealed through the local newspaper in Bolton for anybody who had the ball to let him have it and there would be free beer in the pub he owned in the town. Luckily, it had landed in the lap of a Bolton rather than Manchester United fan and the centre-forward got his memento of the game.

Such was the way the events of the Munich disaster hung over the game that Hartle reveals that he and Tommy Banks nearly didn't bother with the traditional lap of honour for the winners to parade the trophy. "We had been up to get our medals from the Royal Box and we walked back down and stood around and waited for someone to tell us to go on the lap of honour. I looked at Tommy Banks and he asked me what I thought and I said I didn't know. We were both going to walk off into the dressing-room when Bert Sproston, the trainer, came over and told us: 'You must do the lap of honour. It will be the biggest thing in your career and you will remember it all your life.' He was right as it turned out, but at the time we just couldn't see what all the fuss was about. After Munich the match was a bit meaningless I suppose."

The lap of honour sticks in his memory with any doubts disappearing once the players began the journey round the pitch with the Cup and the crowd started cheering. The player is glad he listened to Bert Sproston.

After the disappointment of 1953, Hartle remembers that the return to Bolton this time was a terrific occasion. The bus started out in Manchester and once it reached the far outskirts of Bolton there were crowds lining the streets. They stopped at Kearsley and

Farnworth Town Halls before making their way to the centre of Bolton. The day was full of cherished memories. "When we arrived at Bolton Town Hall, it was wonderful. An absolutely incredible experience. I don't know the official figure for the number of people there, but I have certainly never seen as many people as there were that day. It brought home the difference between winning and losing at Wembley."

Hodgkinson watched the Cup being brought back to Burnden Park with pride, although he, like many Bolton fans, had been upset to learn that the players had been pelted with eggs and fruit by United supporters as they came through Salford on their way from Piccadilly in Manchester. "As they carried the Cup back, I was over the moon. I remembered what had happened five years earlier. The atmosphere was electric and thousands turned out. There were far more Bolton fans at Burnden Park than ever managed to get into Wembley. I must have been there nearly five hours and the celebrations just carried on."

Brandwood was also there for the homecoming. She had been elated at winning the Cup, but there was little time to stay in London to celebrate because the coach was leaving straight after the game, so the homecoming was when the real party could be held, although as a non-drinker she toasted their success with nothing stronger than lemonade. "After being at the Town Hall five years before when everybody was so down this more than made up for it. We cheered and screamed and you could see the players were elated. I was happy for them and it was wonderful; we were all there sharing the success. It was one of my proudest moments."

Both Hopkinson and Banks missed out on the celebrations back at Bolton because they had been called up for England duty and reported to the training headquarters. Banks had already caught the train back home when word was sent ahead and he got off en route and set off for what would be his first cap. He is famously said to have told England manager Walter

Winterbottom on his arrival at the training camp: "Thou's stopped me having a bloody good day back in Bolton. Walter, thou's a lot to answer for."

There was, though, a good celebration after the official banquet at the Café Royal, as Banks fondly recalls. After a League game against Chelsea a few weeks earlier, Banks and some of the Bolton players had gone into the West End for a meal and to visit a nightclub. Brimming with confidence, Banks asked for the manager and told him: "You are talking to the FA Cup winners. We are going to beat Manchester United and afterwards we want a bit of a do here."

The manager was sceptical at first, but some of the staff with more knowledge of football than he had quickly intervened and assured him that this indeed was a party of Bolton Wanderers players and they were in the Final at Wembley. A table for more than twenty to include wives and girl friends was promised. The reservation was secured when Banks rashly promised that not only would the winning team be arriving, they would also be bringing the FA Cup with them!

The official function was at the Café Royal and, maintaining his dislike for the directors and hangers-on surrounding the club, Banks points out that on the official photographs it was hard to make out the players for all the directors and their friends. The players were still having a good time, though, and Hopkinson remembers that by now Banks' unease about winning the Cup in such circumstances and the shadow of the Munich disaster hanging over the game was starting to lift. After all, when it came to football, Bolton knew about defeats. Many had been at the same venue five years earlier when it was the Blackpool players celebrating. Now Banks announced: "The winners can laugh – and the losers can please their bloody selves."

At around midnight it was time to go on to the nightclub Banks had so thoughtfully lined up. Most of the players were there, including Nat Lofthouse who tended to avoid such late-night drinking sessions with his team mates. Banks takes up the story: "When we got there it was jam-packed full of Bolton fans. Whether somebody had passed the word round that we would be there, I don't know. The manager came over and said he hadn't been able to stop them coming into the club, but we were welcome to come in. Nat, in his knowledge, said we should go back to the hotel and have our own do there and so we did.

"Back at the hotel we had a hell of a do. I can't remember much but I know at one point I was drinking champagne out of my wife's shoe and everybody was singing. The coach, George Taylor, and his assistant, Roger Hunt, arrived back and were going to bed and I persuaded them to come and join us and the party carried on. Like a 'Big Time Charlie' I now says to the manager, 'Book all the drinks down to the club.' Most stayed up all night."

He remembers the following day, Lofthouse had his breakfast served in the foyer so he could meet the fans who had called by. Banks says: "It was out of character for him, but he was so elated at winning the Cup. I think of those of us there, he had been the most disappointed when we lost in 1953 and winning had meant so much to him."

It was now the summons arrived for the players to meet manager Bill Ridding. A bar bill for more than £70 had just been presented and an inquest was going to be held. Such an amount represented a huge sum in the late Fifties. Even so, Banks couldn't believe such a fuss was being made when Wanderers had won the Cup for the first time since 1929 and the Wembley gate receipts had been more than £50,000.

In an act of bravado, Banks asked how much exactly the bill was and dismissively said he would pay it, reaching into his pocket where there was just one £5 note. Ridding, though, was shamed into picking up the tab before Banks' bluff was called. The manager did say he wouldn't have minded if he had known and been invited to the party. The last word, of course, went to Banks: "We couldn't invite you because you were all over London partying with the VIPs," he replied.

When he recalls the Final, Lofthouse admits he can't help remembering that League game against Manchester United a few months earlier in the middle of January. Bolton were on the wrong end of a 7-2 hiding. While there might have been no love lost between the fans, the players of the two clubs always got on well. In the United dressing-room were bottled beers and a can opener and Lofthouse went in for a chat and a drink. He joked with the United players that they must have been worried as Bolton had enjoyed a late rally. Sixteen days later, many of those players with whom he had shared a drink were dead.

A Last Hurrah:
1958-60

BUOYED by the success at Wembley and with a settled team in its prime, the 1958-59 season was to be one of the most successful of the decade and yet in many ways for the players and supporters it was ultimately a year that was an anti-climax. A good Cup run ended disappointingly in the sixth round and though a fourth-place finish in the League was the best achieved in the decade, any real challenge for the championship faltered too early.

Roy Hartle remembers: "The Cup-winning team stayed together and we started the season strongly. It was a good year, but it should have been better. We got to the sixth round of the Cup and went out in a game we should have won, and finished fourth in the League, but it was the best chance since the war to win it. We went seven or eight games without defeat. It was a wonderful run and we should have built on it and finished higher in the League than we did."

The Cup holders paraded the trophy before they kicked-off their League campaign of the new season with a four-goal demolition of Leeds United and Nat Lofthouse was again at his best, scoring two of the goals. The first came after 21 minutes to give the crowd something to cheer on a bright sunny

Saturday in August. Stevens and Parry played a one-two before putting Lofthouse through. The centre-forward's second was a shot of such force that the Leeds 'keeper could only knock the ball over his head and into the net. Birch and Parry collected three and four.

Brian Birch was another player whose promise had been identified while he was still young and who was to receive a good grounding in the Bolton reserve team of the mid-Fifties before breaking into the first team in time for the 1958 Final. He had been spotted playing for Southport Boys and was only sixteen when he played his first League game, against Aston Villa in September 1954, as a stand-in for the injured Doug Holden at outside-left. However, he won a regular place in 1957 and played throughout the Cup run where he was the youngest player in the side at Wembley, aged twenty. He remained at Wanderers until 1964, although his appearances in the first team during the later years were infrequent.

The 1958-59 season might have been full of promise, but it was not without its setbacks as well. Bolton may have been performing well and challenging for the title, but a trip to Arsenal for a midweek game on September 9 proved a serious dent to the confidence. Bolton were to finish the League campaign in fourth place, Arsenal a place above them on goal-average. But they seemed worlds apart on this Tuesday night as the home side put six goals past a bewildered Wanderers with a Parry penalty offering little consolation.

As the season opened, though, it proved the only hiccup in an eight-game run without defeat. A 3-2 win over Nottingham Forest at Burnden Park saw the Wanderers in the top of the table. Twice the home side had fallen behind in the first half, but they improved dramatically after the break and at the end, two Lofthouse headers and a Stevens shot were enough to secure the points.

The next game was a home defeat against Burnley and although Wanderers stayed in contention, there were too many reverses to offer a serious title challenge and they finished eleven points adrift of champions Wolverhampton Wanderers. Bolton, though, had the satisfaction of taking three points from their meetings, with a 2-1 away win and a 2-2 draw at Burnden. A run of three defeats in March, when they conceded eleven goals against Blackpool, Aston Villa and West Ham United, proved a serious setback to any lingering hopes of a title chase.

The November 22 win away at Wolves, though, was a performance to savour. Wolves were the reigning champions and had a formidable record against the Wanderers, though Bolton were buoyed by their FA Charity Shield success of the previous month with a 4-1 win at Burnden. In their twelve previous encounters on Wolves' home turf, Bolton had lost nine times and won only once, conceding 39 goals in the process. Wanderers started badly, with the defence lacking confidence, and they conceded an early goal. However, once Stevens had brought the visitors level, it was Wolves who were under the greater pressure and the winning goal came courtesy of Lofthouse. In the second half there were chances for Bolton to extend their lead and Wolves twice cleared off the line with the 'keeper beaten.

While Lofthouse in the white shirt of Bolton might have been in sparkling form, in the white shirt of England things were about to take a turn for the worse. After the Wolves game there was a midweek international against Wales and it was a disappointing display with the Bolton man, in particular, being singled out for criticism. For a player who had, for the most part, enjoyed a good press this was a particularly disappointing time. The verdict in the papers was that the 2-2 draw at Villa Park should bring the curtain down on his international career. It proved to be the case.

The win against Wolves built on the success of the previous week when, on a foggy day, Bolton fans had the satisfaction of a resounding victory over their Cup Final opponents, Manchester United. A great throng of supporters waited outside for the results of a 2pm pitch inspection and it was only twenty minutes later the decision came to allow play. After the wait to get in, such was the extent of the smog that large sections of the crowd were unable to see the nine-goal feast that was laid before them. Six of the goals went to the home side and it was all the more remarkable an effort in that Nat Lofthouse was out injured. His reliable stand-in, Ralph Gubbins, collected two, but those watching found it impossible to say whether they had been scored by head or foot.

Bolton were determined to win a return to Wembley to defend the Cup and away wins at Scunthorpe and a hard-fought encounter with Wolves, which was won 2-1, set up an epic Cup-tie against Preston North End that was to last for three matches and be watched by a total crowd of nearly 150,000.

North End arrived at Burnden Park on February 14, 1959, beset with injuries and on a run of poor form in the League. They were firm underdogs against the reigning Cup holders and a Parry goal after twelve minutes gave the home side a 1-0 lead at the interval. Campbell equalised, only for Birch to restore the lead with just over a quarter of an hour remaining. Preston were fortunate to get a dubious penalty decision that was converted by Thompson, but few could deny they were worth the draw on the day. Nat Lofthouse was said to have told his colleagues afterwards that Bolton couldn't play as poorly as that again, and Preston had played better than anyone expected.

Four days later, the support was such that fans had to be locked outside the Preston ground. Bolton looked to have done enough to clinch the tie, thanks to a first-half Holden goal that saw him dribble around the 'keeper. But the visitors were to pay dearly for a late slip that saw Smith clinch a 89th-minute equaliser. Again, North End had shown great spirit to fight back although Wanderers should have settled the tie at this attempt.

As if the two sides had not already seen enough of each other before the replay at Blackburn Rovers' Ewood Park, the two met in a League fixture. Bolton supporters hoped it would prove an omen as their side won 2-1 with a late Birch goal settling the issue when he beat three defenders with four minutes remaining

When the sides met for the Cup replay, Bolton finally triumphed thanks to a Lofthouse goal. The centre-forward profited from a defensive error to unleash a powerful shot from sixteen yards. This time there was no escape for North End and, in truth, Bolton should have extended their lead. Five hours of fifth-round action had been brought to an end.

Overcoming such a difficult hurdle gave Wanderers fans the hope that the football fates were with them, but in the next round such dreams were to be shattered. A trip to Nottingham Forest proved an insurmountable obstacle with Wanderers going out and ending twelve successive Cup-tie wins. The Forest cause was helped by a goal within five minutes by Tommy Wilson and when Bolton emerged for the second half determined to pull back the deficit, the same player scored a second within three minutes of play resuming. The timing of the goals was a particular blow to the holders and although they pulled one back with a snap goal by Birch, and kept up a barrage of attacks towards the end, they could not get the equaliser they desperately needed. Forest, though, deserved their win and their defenders had got the best over Lofthouse. In truth, Bolton had been lucky not to go further behind. Perhaps the marathon against Preston North End had taken too heavy a toll on the players.

A letter sent by Forest fans to Burnden Park after the game gives an indication of the high regard the players and fans were held in. Sportsmanlike conduct on and off the field has been a virtue of Wanderers down the years and it was certainly not lost on the three fans who took the trouble to write. "May we three Nottingham Forest supporters who attended the Cup-tie with Bolton Wanderers express our admiration of the way in which your team accepted defeat and the sportsmanship of the players during the game. Wanderers supporters, too, must be among the very best in football. We talked to quite a few before and during the game and, believe us, it was a pleasure to talk to them."

Before a disappointing run of defeats finally ended any League hopes there was a resounding victory against Chelsea with Hill scoring a hat-trick and Lofthouse bagging a brace in a 6-0 win. It was the perfect antidote to the disappointment of the Cup defeat a week earlier. It also fuelled the exasperation of Wanderers fans at their team's ability to play football that reached such giddy heights one week, only to slump into the abyss the next. The win was sandwiched between that Cup defeat and a 4-0 hiding at Blackpool.

There were hopes that the 1959-60 season would be the chance to build on the success of the previous year. Fans were now getting used to vying for honours and saw a future that was bright. It was, though, to prove the last of the salad days before the grim reality of the early Sixties was ushered in. The bulk of the great Cup-winning side were still in place, but the signs that the beginning of the end was not far away were already evident. Wanderers would limp out of the FA Cup in the fourth round to West Bromwich Albion, 2-0, after having needed a replay to account for close neighbours Bury in the third round.

The Bury fixture was perhaps an indication of fading glories, although the old adage that the Cup is a great leveller certainly holds true. Bury arrived as the Bolton side were in their best League form and when Third Division opposition should have been a mere hors d'oeuvres for greater things to come, but the lowly side managed a 1-1 draw before the best-ever crowd seen at Gigg Lane of 35,000.

Wanderers fans were convinced the return at Burnden Park would be a formality, but it proved far from the case. Stevens gave the home side the lead with a short-range header from Hill's centre, but Bury drew level and then took the lead when Watson forced the ball home after being left unmarked at a corner. On a snow-covered pitch, Bury players ignored any thoughts of their own wellbeing and looked the more composed. With fifteen minutes left, Holden put Parry clear and he jinked his way past three opponents before slotting home the goal that tied the game in normal time. Bolton's blushes had been saved and two extra-time goals finally saw the side through, but it was unconvincing.

For the next round of the FA Cup, against West Bromwich Albion, a fleet of coaches took hundreds of fans to the Midlands for a tie that was expected to be close. In the event there could be no complaints at a 2-0 reverse. Despite a Hennin tackle, Jackson managed to get his shot away to give the home side an early lead before Wanderers had the chance to settle. Bolton had few chances, with the best falling to Stevens who collected a Holden cross but fired his shot wide. It was a miss the visitors were to regret. The ball-playing Davey Burnside clinched it for West Brom when he nutmegged a defender before hitting a terrific shot from just inside the penalty box. Hopkinson got his finger tips to the ball but it went in off the inside of the post. The players felt they had let down the large contingent who had travelled down to support them.

In the League, two defeats in the opening two fixtures of the season in Lancashire derbies against Blackpool and Blackburn Rovers did not augur well for any championship aspirations. However, victories in the last three fixtures of the season brought a respectable sixth place in the table. The biggest victory, though, had come much earlier in the campaign, back in September when West Ham went down by 5-1 and there was that rarest of sights; a Tommy Banks goal. In 255 League and Cup appearances for Wanderers, he scored only twice and, despite having made his first appearance in the 1947-48 season, this was his first goal for the club – and having been so long in coming it was at least a sterling effort. He recalls the game was played in glorious sunshine and with an hour gone the scores were level with a goal by Hill being cancelled by West Ham with a Vic Keeble equaliser two minutes before the interval. A rare venture upfield saw him hit one of those shots that so often end high in the terracing, but on this occasion it crashed into the roof of the net. Two goals for Neville Bannister and one for Stevens as the clock ticked down ensured a runaway victory.

There was, though, a worrying sign for the directors and those involved with the club's finances. The Burnden Park faithful were beginning to vote with their feet as they became disillusioned with their side promising much but failing to deliver. For the first home game of the season, against Blackburn Rovers, more than 42,324 had packed the stands and terraces. By the last home match, against Chelsea, the attendance was down to 19,432. On that day only two First Division games had less support. Those who did turn up, though, were treated to a 2-0 win against a side who lost goalkeeper Peter Bonetti after thirty minutes. Two second-half goals by Birch and Hill settled proceedings.

Florence Brandwood recalls that in these seasons the fans got happily used to their side being among the best in the country and although there were disappointments there were some great games and good football. "We never thought it would end. Throughout the decade, players had gone through injury and retirement, but there were always others waiting to take their place. It never crossed our minds that this process would stop. We assumed we would always be near to the top and dreamt that one day the ultimate prize of a League championship would be ours. What we couldn't imagine was how quickly the decline would come."

Throughout much of the season injuries deprived Bolton of the services of Bryan Edwards, Tommy Banks and Eddie Hopkinson for long periods. Most importantly, though, Nat Lofthouse missed the entire season, having been injured on a pre-season tour to South Africa. The absence of the star centre-forward meant only Nottingham Forest and Luton Town scored fewer goals in the League – a poor goalscoring return that a fit Lofthouse would undoubtedly have rectified. In defence Bolton maintained their tradition of being strong, with only Tottenham Hotspur having a better record. What the injuries also highlighted, though, was the lack of quality in depth at the club. A handful of players held the key to success and injury or retirement to them would see Wanderers struggle unless adequate replacements were found. As the new decade dawned, changes in football in general and a period of transition at the club would see it becoming increasingly difficult to fill the gaps left by experienced stalwarts.

The Beginning of the End

THE Sixties dawned and with it came the harsh reality of life in a new era. While the Fifties closed with Wanderers supporters disappointed that the championship challenge had faltered, now it was to be a return to the days of relegation dogfights. As the Cup-winning side began to break up, the handful of veterans who remained attempted to coax the best out of some inexperienced youngsters who replaced them.

Indeed, it could be argued that these first few seasons brought out the finest performances in the old guard, without whose efforts the body blow of relegation would have been delivered far sooner than in the 1963-64 season. Eddie Hopkinson recalls: "I remember some of the early seasons in the Sixties as among my best. We were up against it and it was the efforts of some of the more experienced players who helped us through. We may have only just avoided relegation on a couple of occasions, but that was an achievement in itself."

But he believes Bolton's hopes were undermined by the decision to sell players who still had much to offer and for whom he could see no players of the same calibre ready to take over. It was a short-term measure for financial reasons that made no sense. And now the much-vaunted scouting system was not producing the crop of richly talented players that had been Wanderers great strength. This was no fault of the system. Such things are cyclical. Bolton had benefited when there was a rich seam of talent to be tapped. Now the quality was just not there.

An answer might have been the age-old question for Bolton of going out to buy. They didn't, of course, to any serious extent. Hopkinson says: "One of Tommy Banks' favourite sayings was where has all the money gone? There was a lot of money coming into the club with people paying 7s 6d in the stand and the players on the maximum wage. I'd love to know where it all went."

Players like Dennis Stevens, Ray Parry and Doug Holden were lost. Tommy Banks left and Hopkinson has nothing but the highest praise for the full-back as a team man. "You couldn't get big-headed or over-confident because Tommy would knock you down straight away, but he was wonderful at building you up. Everybody from the 1958 team keeps in touch and Tommy does the organ-ising. If you get the message there is a function on, you have to be there. It's like a Royal Command when Tommy gets in contact."

Banks also cannot believe that such quality players were allowed to depart. "Ray Parry and Dennis Stevens were the engine-room of the side. Everybody talks about Lofty, myself and Roy Hartle, but those two ran their legs off every week. Doug Holden was another most underrated player. I don't know what was in their minds when they let such players go."

Parry was transferred to Blackpool in October 1960 and after four years moved to Bury where he made his League debut ironically against Bolton. He celebrated his 500th League game in 1968 and just to prove to those who let him go that there was still life in the legs, he played on with Bury until 1972. In March 1962, Stevens was sold for the then-largest incoming fee Bolton had received – £35,000 – to move to Everton. Again to underline the view of Banks and Hopkinson, a further 120 League games for the

Merseysiders, including a championship medal in 1963, showed that he could still perform at the highest level. He played for both Oldham Athletic and Tranmere Rovers before retiring in 1968 with a back injury. After eleven seasons as a first-team regular with Bolton, Holden left in November 1962, joining Preston with whom he played in the 1964 FA Cup Final, scoring a goal in their 3-2 defeat by West Ham.

Roy Hartle remembers the early seasons of the decade were when the Cup-winning team began to break up with probably half a dozen going by 1961. The retirement of Nat Lofthouse was a blow to the team and Hartle believes the couple of players Wanderers bought to try to give the youngsters coming through some experience didn't come up to expectations. "I could see the writing on the wall halfway through the 1961-62 season. I was captain from 1961 until 1966 and it was not a particularly good time for myself. We lost too many players all at once. We were a First Division side suddenly fielding young boys who weren't ready for that level of football. It was asking boys to do a man's job. We struggled from day one. It was hard work for myself and Eddie Hopkinson because we were the mainstay of the side."

Tommy Banks remembers this was also a period of militancy among players as the beginning of the push that would eventually lead to the abolition of the minimum wage began to take effect. He recalls a large meeting organised by the Professional Footballers' Association in Manchester where there were 400 people in attendance and the vote was overwhelming in favour of a strike by the players. Banks, though, believes that at Bolton they should have pressed sooner in the late Fifties when the team was strong and the crowds large and there was a considerable degree of bargaining power at the players' disposal. If they could have all been prepared to exercise it.

He said: "That was when they should have sorted this contract business out, when the players had the upper hand and there were large crowds generating the money. Not just at Bolton but throughout the League. That was when we should have universally gone for better money. Why we didn't go for that I don't know."

As it was, by 1961 Banks' days at the club were numbered. There was his outspoken views on players' rights, coupled with a problem with pulled muscles, and so at 31 he departed for non-League football with Altrincham. To support his views on the poor deal professional footballers were getting at this time, he points out he was earning more money playing non-League football and working in the building trade than in his heyday at Burnden Park. His appreciation of the Professional Footballers' Association remains undimmed and they have helped him since. After a lifetime of football and then hod-carrying on building sites, he needed hip replacements and the union helped pay towards the cost.

The first season of the decade began with Wanderers failing to notch a victory in their first four matches, before new signing Irish international Bill McAdams began to repay his £15,000 transfer fee to Manchester City. He sparked a second-half rally against Chelsea that brought a first win for Wanderers in thirty hours of football. The visitors were leading at half-time, thanks to a goal by the great Jimmy Greaves. Then came the fightback and McAdams was instrumental in both opening goals by Holden and Edwards. The centre-forward, playing in place of the injured Lofthouse, collected the next two himself when he hit a first-time shot after receiving a through ball from Hill, and five minutes from the end scored with a flick from a Hill cross. A 4-1 victory promised hope for the future and McAdams looked as though he might solve the goalscoring problems created by the absence of Lofthouse. However, despite scoring 26 goals in 44 League appearances, he stayed just over a season before joining Leeds United.

At Burnden Park, McAdams got his chance to answer a crisis at centre-forward. When Lofthouse missed the previous season after injuring himself on a club tour to South Africa, such was the paucity of resources that Dennis Stevens was drafted in as a centre-forward and to his credit scored fifteen times. On a couple of occasions, though, the number-nine shirt was handed to centre-half Derek Hennin, now nearing the end of his career at Wanderers.

Bolton finished the season only three points clear of the relegation zone and that was plainly too close for comfort. A measure of the fans' apathy was an attendance of only 12,637 for the last game of the season when Bolton could manage only a draw with Preston North End who were already doomed to Division Two football. These were opposition who, only a few years before, had attracted crowds of around 50,000 for some thrilling Cup-ties. There was no Cup glory for Bolton this season. In the FA Cup, a fourth-round draw with Blackburn Rovers at Burnden Park was followed by a 4-0 exit in the replay at Ewood Park.

The season marked the beginning of the League Cup competition and a clear indication of its popularity among the fans was that only 11,000 turned out for a replay against Hull City to see McAdams notch the first Bolton goal in the competition after only four minutes with a well-directed header from a Birch cross. The final score was 5-1 to the home side with the highlight being McAdams' second and Bolton's fifth when he dribbled thorough a posse of defenders before drawing the 'keeper, beating his lunge at the ball and then sliding it into an undefended net. Such moments in the competition were to be shortlived as Rotherham unceremoniously dumped the First Division side out of the competition with a 2-0 win at Burnden and reality again reared its ugly head. A crowd of only 6,594 showed what the fans thought of the new competition and Bolton's performances.

A 3-1 win over Manchester City in November 1960 provided only the fourth win of the season and marked the first full-team appearance of 16-year-old Francis Lee. He had played only eight Central League games before being given his chance in the first team while still an amateur and marked the occasion with a goal when Lofthouse and McAdams could not get on the end of a Stevens centre and the youngster headed the ball into the net off the foot of a post. Lee also managed to collect a booking. It would not be the first in the long career that lay ahead of him. A Stanley free-kick that took a deflection provided the home side's first goal and Lofthouse made the points secure with a header from Lee's corner. It would be the last League goal scored by Lofthouse at Burnden Park.

However, what was more indicative of Bolton's form was highlighted with the arrival of Burnley at Burnden Park. While in previous seasons Wanderers' home form had helped keep the club in the upper reaches of the League, there was now a worrying slump. Reigning champions Burnley were to win 5-3 as the home defence conceded too many chances to a side well equipped to take advantage of such largesse. Typical was a poor back pass to Hopkinson that let in Connelly for Burnley's second. With Pointer also collecting two for the visitors, Bolton were always chasing the game. At half-time they were 3-1 down and three minutes after the restart Pointer crossed low and Robson converted. Two late Bolton goals, by Lee and McAdams, were never going to alter the result and merely made the scoreline look more respectable by adding to McAdams' first half score.

On a black day for the Bolton club, the Wanderers travelled to Birmingham City on December 17 and salvaged a point thanks to two Stevens goals when the visitors were reduced to ten men. What marks the occasion out, though, was that the reason the Bolton side were depleted was due to an injury to Nat Lofthouse that effectively ended his career. With City leading 2-1 at half-time, it was Bolton who were beginning to have the better chances when disaster struck. An accurate centre by Lee was met by a Birch header and as the 'keeper Withers went to make the catch, he was challenged by Lofthouse. Both men fell heavily and it was clear the centre-forward had badly twisted his knee.

Florence Brandwood remembers seeing players from both sides crowding round him and sensing this was serious. The players were joined by all three officials and when manager Bill Ridding came out, the worst was feared. The Burnden Park legend left on a stretcher and Brandwood says she feared that, given the player's recent injury problems, it might be the end of his career. It proved the case, although Lofthouse did attempt a shortlived comeback the following season.

Gordon Taylor had not needed much encouragement to join the team he had supported from boyhood and he was particularly keen having seen Wanderers achieve Wembley success in 1958 with a largely home-grown team. He felt if he was going to make it as a professional footballer, then he would have the best chance at Burnden Park.

He was not the only talented youngster to join at that time. Francis Lee had just arrived and was already full of confidence. Taylor remembers being in a café across from the ground with Lee when the two discussed whether they would sign professional forms. Taylor's mind was already made up. The precocious Lee announced that he, too, would join because he had seen the first team and was confident he would be in it by the end of the season. Of course he was.

Lofthouse departed, leaving an England forward of the future to take centre stage. Francis Lee was the exception that proved the rule when the question of the quality of youngsters now coming through the Bolton ranks was raised. He was to enjoy eight seasons at Burnden Park that were frequently dogged with controversy. He was not one to take adversity lightly either on or off the field. Bookings were the outcome on the field of play. Off it, Bill Ridding had to deal with a young player who did not take kindly to being left out of the side. He was the Wanderers' top scorer for five seasons until he left to join Manchester City in September 1967 for a fee of £65,000. At Maine Road he went on to win both the League and Cup as well as playing 27 times for England, including the 1970 World Cup in Mexico.

With Lofthouse gone and Dennis Stevens moving to centre-forward, the way was open for Freddie Hill to establish a place in the Wanderers' front line. Hill had turned down offers to sign for Sheffield Wednesday in his home town and joined Wanderers in 1957. He was an inside-forward who regularly scored goals, hitting the net seven times in only eighteen League appearances in the 1958-59 season. Hill was picked for England in October 1962, against Northern Ireland, and was to win one more international cap. He was never fully settled at Burnden Park and between 1962 and 1964, four times put in transfer requests. At one point Liverpool agreed a £60,000 transfer fee, but Hill failed the medical with high blood pressure. He eventually left Bolton in July 1969 when he joined Halifax Town for a £5,000 fee.

Taylor remembers that the highly-acclaimed talent spotting system at Burnden Park was fallible. Another youngster there at the same time was not so fortunate in making the grade and was released. His name was Alan Ball, the same player who would later collect a World Cup winners' medal with England.

The 1961-62 season saw a gradual improvement with an eleventh place finish in the League, thanks to an impressive late flourish which saw four wins and two draws in the last six games of the season and included a 6-1 demolition of Nottingham Forest. However, Bolton's great Cup tradition again deserted them as they went out in the third round of the FA Cup to Manchester United, 2-1 at Old Trafford, and in the League Cup were held to a 1-1 draw at Burnden by Sunderland and then lost the replay to the only goal of the match. The hopes of the fans were that the team could take heart from the fine way they finished the season and maintain that at the start of the new campaign.

Bolton went the first three games without defeat, but it was to be a false dawn. For the next seven games there were six defeats and the only win again confirmed their status as a bogey team for

Manchester United, who were beaten 3-0. Such victories, though, were rare and only two wins late in the season, against Leicester City and Liverpool, kept them clear of relegation trouble. Even so, eighteenth place in the table again did not bode well. The team also exited from both Cup competitions at the first hurdle, against Sheffield United in the FA Cup and a 4-0 hammering away to Norwich City in the League Cup. The transitional nature of the side and the need to throw young players into first-team football was highlighted by a League game against Sheffield United in March 1963. Wanderers fielded their youngest-ever forward line: Lee (18), Hill (23), Davies (20), Bromley (16) and Butler (18). Roy Hartle's fears that boys were being asked to do men's jobs was graphically illustrated in the medium term, although a 3-2 win that day, with a hat-trick from Freddie Hill, tempers the point. Yet in fairness to the club's officials, when they had bought, then the players recruited had proved disappointing including Brian Pilkington from Burnley and Ron McGarry from Workington.

The youngsters had their moments as we have seen. They occasionally gave a glimmer of what Wanderers were capable of when everything clicked with their young side. They were able to bounce back from a 5-0 reverse against Aston Villa to take the points against a quality Tottenham Hotspur in December 1962. The crowd were given something to cheer when Hill beat a Norman tackle and passed wide to Denis Butler. His pass towards goal was taken by Lee, whose clever shot towards goal was saved by Brown. The 'keeper was called into action minutes later, to turn a good shot by Davies round for a corner. Brown had the most work to do, although Hopkinson had to be alert to stop a chance from Greaves. Spurs gained the upper hand as the match wore on, but were unable to turn their pressure into goals. With five minutes remaining, Bolton scored the only goal of the match when Hill found Deakin and he beat a defender before firing home. It would be more than two months before the next home game as the big freeze set in and lasted until the beginning of March.

By the time Gordon Taylor made his debut, in a 4-0 reverse against Wolverhampton in March 1963, he could sense there were difficult times ahead. Many of the old stalwarts like Eddie Hopkinson, Doug Holden and Roy Hartle had seen their best days. Lofthouse had been forced into retirement through injury and players like Tommy Banks had departed. Taylor went into the team when things were, in his words, pretty bleak and that game against Wolves was not the most auspicious of starts. He remembers before the kick-off hoping he wouldn't let anybody down.

Tom Hodgkinson watching from the terraces said it was obvious that the team was starting to struggle as the side of the late Fifties started to break up and the players being brought in didn't seem as good and there was suddenly an unsettled look about it all. "The players who had served so well were getting past their best as they grew old together. Among the fans the talk was that we should have got some quality new players in. The club seemed to get left behind when the maximum wage was abolished."

He recalls that after the excitement of the late Fifties, now it was hard to pick a game out from the memory among the weekly grind of League matches, many of which were being lost to sides who would once have provided easy points. These were seasons when Bolton were never in contention for anything and the form was woefully inconsistent.

New players were drafted in to try to stop the rot and some, like Warwick Rimmer and Wyn Davies, would later be mainstays at the club as it struggled in the lower divisions before re-emerging in the Seventies. Rimmer was born in Tranmere and had signed as an amateur in 1956 after excelling for England Schoolboys. He turned professional in March 1958 and made his debut in the League Cup in 1960-61. He made only two appearances that season. The following year he was a regular in the half-back line and although his career began in the First Division he was to be in the side during two relegations, although he captained the side that won the Third Division championship in 1973. He left in March 1975, joining Crewe. By then he had played 521 League and Cup games for Wanderers.

Wyn Davies was a £20,000 signing from Wrexham in March 1962, to answer a crisis at centre-forward, and he was to be a regular for four and a half years. Dubbed by the fans, "Wyn the leap" because of his skill in the air, he won sixteen caps for Wales while with Bolton and went on to win 34 in total. He moved to Newcastle United in October 1966 for £80,000 and was to have spells at both Manchester clubs, Blackpool, Crystal Palace and Stockport County before ending his League career at Crewe in 1977. In 170 League and Cup appearances for Wanderers, he scored 74 goals.

Many of the new recruits were to spend much of their time at Wanderers plying their trade in the lower divisions. The fears expressed by Roy Hartle at the start of the decade about Bolton's future in the First Division were now about to be realised. Their escape from the drop in 1962-63 was to be the last such cliff hanger they would survive. Fate was to take a hand and deliver a cruel blow.

Relegation and the Wilderness Beckons

HAVING finished in eighteenth place in the First Division twice in the previous three seasons, it came as no surprise to Bolton fans that their side would again be involved in a battle to avoid relegation. Given the squad had not been strengthened since the previous season, and experienced campaigners Eddie Hopkinson and Roy Hartle were a year older, there was little to persuade people through the turnstiles, and attendances again suffered. Yet although 1963-64 would prove the relegation season and see the club slide into obscurity, a late rally gave hope of survival and at the end of it Wanderers could consider themselves unlucky.

Only four victories in the opening 26 League and Cup games of the season appeared to make relegation a certainty. The depths to which Wanderers had slipped were brutally brought home when Blackburn Rovers arrived at Burnden on February 29 and promptly handed out a five-goal drubbing. It is a measure of the club's decline that such a reverse was not even deemed a shock, even though it was the heaviest home defeat in eleven years. Such was the level of form that the team had slipped to. It hardly needs repeating that the call from the terraces was for the club to spend its way out of trouble with one or two big-name signings. As the side reached its nadir, though, there was a view voiced that it would need at least half a dozen new players to bring about a major change. As the campaign wore on, some fans were even taking the heretical view that a short spell in the Second Division to rebuild would be the best option. They thought such an experience would be shortlived. It was to prove a very wrong assumption.

In the Blackburn game, the chief tormentor of the Bolton defenders was centre-forward Fred Pickering, who scored twice and made another and asked questions of a suspect defence for which they held no answers. With a 2-0 lead at half-time, thanks to Pickering and a Ferguson goal when he dribbled round Hopkinson to slide the ball home, the visitors always looked comfortable and two goals within a two-minute spell in the second half ensured Bolton morale would suffer a serious dent. Sadly for Wanderers, Rovers were too strong in every department, although the home side did squander early chances with two shots saved off the line.

With the League form in the doldrums, there was hope that a good Cup campaign would revive fans' interest. The need for a replay to dispose of non-League Bath City did not augur well, but the next round pitted Wanderers against Preston North End and brought back memories of earlier epic Cup encounters between the two clubs. This was their third post-war meeting and a win would have been a hat-trick for Wanderers. Their most notable earlier success had come in the 1958 Cup-winning year when Preston were beaten at Deepdale in the third round. The following year, Wanderers also triumphed in a marathon that took three matches to decide.

Preston were now in the Second Division, but had already

dispatched opposition from the higher league in Nottingham Forest after a replay. Bolton's most experienced back, Roy Hartle, was missing after suffering an eye injury while playing with his four-year-old son. The opening game at Burnden Park also saw the return of an old favourite with Doug Holden now playing for North End. The game was expected to be close and so it proved with Preston taking a two-goal lead, but then Bolton fighting back in a match that was in the great tradition of the Cup. Two goals by the often-criticised Deakin brought Wanderers level and earned a replay.

The winner of the replay faced a home draw against Carlisle United and it was to be Preston who went through. In a game played at a terrific pace, it was the home side who went ahead when Edwards slipped as he went to intercept a through pass and Dawson took advantage. Ten minutes after the break, Wanderers were level when, from a corner by Taylor, it was Edwards who got the header to make amends for his earlier slip. The winning goal was scored by captain Lawton who forced the ball over the line over winger Hatton's falling body. Hatton was injured in the collision and it forced a reshuffle in the Bolton ranks with Lee coming back into defence. In the game's closing seconds, Preston cleared the ball off the line to ensure their win. North End would go all the way to Wembley that year, only to lose the Final to West Ham United.

In the League, when all seemed lost Bolton did give themselves a chance of avoiding the drop with a rally that began at Easter. The beginning of the change in form came with a home draw against Aston Villa, but it was a measure of the supporters' lack of faith that it was played before the lowest crowd of the season with only 8,348 paying customers. Falling crowds presented another dilemma for the club. Without the guaranteed revenue which large attendances bring, and in the new free market created by the abolition of the maximum wage, those in charge of the purse strings now worried whether the club could afford the large transfer fees and wages for players that were being commanded. Their critics would no doubt argue that they had left it too late to be worrying about such matters.

Now showing the same fighting spirit that had been exhibited earlier in the season in their Cup match with Preston, the Bolton players began to enjoy a change in fortune. A 2-1 win over Burnley began the revival. Burnley arrived full of confidence and took the game to Wanderers who relied on attacking on the break. It produced two goals for the home side. The first, after ten minutes, came when a Davison shot was parried and Hatton was on hand with the follow-up shot, despite three defenders on the line. It helped calm Bolton nerves. The second came when a poor back pass was seized on by Hill, who presented Lee with the simplest of chances. The home side then needed to withstand a Burnley fightback which saw Irvine at inside-right head home a cross from the right to narrow the deficit before the break. In the end, Wanderers were just able to hold out and the final whistle came as a relief to Bolton players and fans alike.

The next big test in Bolton's Easter roller-coaster ride, following an away draw with Burnley, was a journey to London to play Cup Finalists West Ham United, who had lost only one of their previous five games. It was another must-win game for the Wanderers, but with their League position seemingly hopeless, the team were now playing with a freedom and confidence lacking earlier in the season. Even so, only the most optimistic Bolton fan could expect a win. Their hopes rested, not so much on the ability of their own side, but the possibility that West Ham players might have their attention focused on their trip to Wembley rather than the more mundane matter of League football. Bolton twice came from behind on a muddy pitch to level the scores by half-time with Bromley netting the decider in a 3-2 win that suddenly held out the promise of an eleventh-hour escape from relegation. Wanderers had four games left and only one point separated them from fellow relegation candidates Birmingham City. Three of those Bolton games were at home and would take on the air of Cup-ties as the end-of-season excitement mounted.

Brian Bromley would add to the goal he scored against West Ham by hitting the net in the next two games – goals that were to prove vital to Bolton's survival chances. Bromley had come through the club's youth system after being seen playing for Burnley Schools at inside-forward, and such was the pressure on Wanderers' playing resources he was given his first outing for the club at the age of just 16, in March 1963, against Sheffield United in Bolton's youngest-ever forward line. It was the first home game in three months because of the big freeze and a Freddie Hill hat-trick saw the home side win 3-2. Bromley played only two more games that season but was back in the side for the 1963-64 campaign and has the distinction of scoring Bolton's last League goal in the First Division until their return to the top-flight fifteen years later. He stayed with the club until he was sold to Portsmouth in November 1969, for £25,000. He ended his career, in March 1975 at Darlington, where he had gone on loan.

For Florence Brandwood, doing the calculations to see how many points would bring safety had begun early in the season. Like compulsive gamblers, committed fans work out every permutation, grasp at any possible straws and hold out hope until it is mathematically impossible for the side to survive. Ifs and buts litter the conversation and they wager no end of emotion, despite knowing there is little chance of a return.

Brandwood said: "The season had gone badly and the players were just not as good as the ones that went before. By Easter it looked all over, but we never gave up hope and then there was a typical late Wanderers rally to keep us on the edge of our seats. I really thought we could do it and if we had stayed up the team might have started to gel and maybe we could have survived."

Bert Gregory had seen the good times and was now witnessing one of the lows. This was not the club he had admired for so long and he says disparagingly of the players who were now wearing the white shirts of Wanderers: "Generally they were not performing. Some of them couldn't even throw-in properly. You could see the difficulties ahead and now the team, which once never changed, was now never settled. You can never have a winning team if you change every match."

Gregory says the coach, George Taylor, had asked him for his verdict when the team were anchored to the bottom. His response was simple: "I told him, if they don't buck their ideas up we will go down. They looked as though they didn't want to play. It was a far cry from the teams of the Fifties. They were hard players."

The relegation season was Michael Walker's first when he was a regular supporter at Burnden Park. Aged thirteen, he would travel with three or four friends the short journey from his home to the ground either by bus or sometimes, to save money, they would walk. He remembers the excitement and sense of responsibility in being allowed to go on his own to watch the Wanderers. The results, though, were not so wonderful.

"I suppose it was just my luck to start supporting the side when they were on the slide," he said. "For us as kids it was a great day out. The glory years that had just gone were not something we even thought about. Our heroes were Warwick Rimmer, Wyn Davies and, of course, Franny Lee. There was an advert for eggs at the time and it was borrowed for a football chant: 'E for B and Franny Lee'. We were aware of players like Nat Lofthouse, but we had never seen him play and he wasn't one of our favourites. From the Fifties the only player I remember was Roy Hartle because he was still playing and was still a tough character. If a winger got past him once he didn't get past a second time, that's for sure."

With the results starting to go badly, the youngster feared the worst. Certainly there was an air of pessimism amongst the older supporters with whom they stood on the terraces. The talk was that buying a couple of quality players would make all the difference. They never arrived. "Through the years, the fans have always called for the club to buy good players, but they have always spent too little and too late. They still manage to charge top prices, though. At the time it didn't matter because we were young and football was everything. It would be another couple of decades before I became disillusioned with football and Wanderers."

He remembers that Wanderers fans that season had to be keen and enthusiastic. By Christmas the side had won only three games, one of them an out-of-character 6-0 trouncing of Ipswich Town. Not suprisingly, the East Anglian club would finish bottom of the table. The issue at stake was who would join them in Division Two. Walker remembers a veteran Wanderers fan joking after such a comfortable win that it wasn't the Bolton team that had run out but a team of ringers, recruited for the day from a local Sunday league. Reality quickly returned as the defeats mounted and Wanderers looked destined for Second Division football.

Walker adds: "Just when it seemed all hope had gone, I remember being at Burnden and Franny Lee got the winner against Burnley. Whether the players thought there was nothing else for it but to go out and give it a go, I don't know. Suddenly we started winning and the late rally had everybody talking. It looked as though we might just scrape clear of the relegation zone."

With just four games to go, Bill Ridding was also starting to believe that a Houdini-style escape might be possible. He warned the fans that there were tough games ahead, but added that the players were now a lot more confident after their recent run of success and were determined to sustain it. He urged the fans to play their part in encouraging the team from the terraces, pointing out that young players especially respond to such support, just as they are easily put down by criticism. He acknowledged that Bolton fans had not had much to cheer for a few seasons, but now was a chance to really let themselves go, and public support would be a big factor in keeping First Division football in the town.

Sheffield United were the opponents in the first of the crucial home games. A win would take Bolton above Birmingham and Roy Hartle remembers the feeling among players was that it would be a huge psychological blow if they could peg Birmingham back into one of the relegation positions. It would mean the Midlanders could have some of the worry that the Bolton players had shouldered in recent weeks. There was also a feeling in the dressing-room that everybody was determined to fight to the last gasp.

Nerves, though, took their toll on Wanderers first-half performance as the occasion was too much for some of the players. The home side were guilty of too many errors, but just before the interval Hill got the vital breakthrough. In truth, it was against the run of play and Sheffield were producing the better football, but the fans didn't care and the sense of relief on the terraces was obvious. The visitors didn't make the most of their chances to draw level and when a Bromley cross was not cleared by Sheffield defenders, Lee put it away to give a valuable breathing space. With the game already won, Bromley got the third. The delight of the supporters was clear as young fans ran on to the field to cheer the players.

Next to visit Burnden Park was Chelsea, who were competing for a top-three League place and had inflicted a 4-0 defeat on Wanderers at Stamford Bridge earlier in the season. They were to find themselves up against a far different team this time. The personnel may have been largely the same, but now the side was playing with a determination and confidence previously lacking. One goal was enough to secure the vital points, scored by Bromley after thirty minutes. The result may have owed more to hard graft than consummate skill, but the defence gave Chelsea few goalscoring opportunities and the excitement was enough to see youngsters back on the field celebrating. With Birmingham defeated at home by Stoke City, Wanderers were now three points clear of them, but had played a game more.

Unbelievably, Wanderers now travelled to Tottenham Hotspur as favourites to win the match given the recent surge in form and Spurs having won only one of their last seven games. It was, though, to be the home side who triumphed by a single goal and a six-match unbeaten run by Bolton had come to an end. There was still confidence among the squad, though, because Birmingham had to win against the newly-crowned League champions Liverpool in midweek or be relegated. Overturning the form book they triumphed 3-1 and Bolton could only wonder what the result might have been if Liverpool had still needed League points to clinch the title.

That result and the defeat at Spurs on the penultimate game of the season meant a point from Bolton's home game against Wolves would still be enough to guarantee survival. Telegrams and messages of good luck began arriving at the ground for the Friday evening fixture. Birmingham City would play the following day. Supporters turned their minds back to the thrilling Cup match against Wolves in 1958, which Wanderers had won against the odds and which had been a major hurdle to overcome on their way to Wembley and Cup glory. The fates, though, were already working against the home side. Freddie Hill was ruled out with a thigh injury and, as if to taunt the relegation-haunted club, the visitors were parading recently-acquired talent in their forward line having recruited Ray Crawford from Ipswich Town, Dick Le Flem from Nottingham Forest and Jimmy Melia from Liverpool. What wouldn't Wanderers fans have given for their club to have the resources to go out and buy.

A sign of the times saw Bolton director Will Hayward attend a meeting of the Football League's club chairmen in the week before the final game of the season. The discussions centred on finding a compromise on wages that would be more in keeping with the majority of clubs' ability to pay and would stop the rich clubs getting richer at the expense of their poorer neighbours, who would inevitably lose out. A suggestion was to reimpose the maximum wage with the amount paid varying on the division and with some form of compromise that rewarded top players and the length of service a player had with a club. Although Bolton and other clubs in a similar situation strongly argued their case, it fell on deaf ears and there was to be no lifeline from this quarter for Bolton and the other East Lancashire clubs.

On the field there was to be no mercy shown either. The all-important League game with Wolves arrived and was understandably tense, although after two minutes Davison squandered an easy chance that would have calmed the side and perhaps altered the whole balance of the game. His shot flew wide and it was Wolves who went ahead after 25 minutes when a Flowers shot could only be parried by Hopkinson, and Crawford converted the simplest of chances. Lee mistimed a shot in the early stages of the second half that would have brought the home side level and two goals in as many minutes ensured a Wolves victory. An injury to Bromley meant Bolton were effectively down to ten men, and a fourth Wolves goal in the 85th minute rubbed salt into the Bolton wounds.

Bolton's fate was now out of their own hands. The day after the Wolves match, Birmingham had to win at home to Sheffield United to save their First Division status and ensure Bolton's relegation. It meant it was the closest possible finish after 42 League games. A 3-0 win against a side reduced to ten men proved comfortable enough in the end for the Midlands side. Bolton's late charge, which saw them having only gained 23 points up to February 17 and then finish on 42 thanks to nineteen points from the last fifteen games proved not quite enough in the end and Bolton's 29-year spell in the top flight was over.

Gregory remembers: "It was very depressing. The players just sat in the dressing-room and didn't speak. They took it very hard. There was nothing anybody could do. The players had done their best and there was no point calling them. It was a season when, even if they played well, they still lost. There were a good few in the dressing-room didn't deserve to lose."

Afterwards the players felt numb and hurt. Roy Hartle said: "I will never forget the Wolves game if I live to be 150. They had a good side and it was terrible for us. It was the most dreadful night. I remember going off at half-time and we were down and thinking this is a game we have to win, and trying to raise the players. At the end it was devastating. We had been in the First Division for years and to be captain of the side when it was relegated didn't go down well. At Easter, the position had looked hopeless and if we had gone down then, before we started collecting points, we would have been prepared for it. After the fightback it was hard to accept. One week earlier we had looked near-certainties to stay up.

"It was very difficult facing the people in Bolton. All sports people are the same. We carried the fans' hopes and dreams and to have been relegated I took very personally and was very upset. I had been in the side for over ten years. I tried to think of what I could say to the fans – but there is nothing you can say.

"One thing about Bolton fans, though, and I think it is why they think the 1958 side is so special, is that if they think you are making an effort and really trying then they will forgive you playing a bad game. The whole 1958 side went out on the field and gave 100 per cent week in week out and for season after season. Those same fans, though, have no real time for you if they don't think you're really bothered."

Bill Ridding said it had been a wonderful fight by the players to get back into the reckoning and he was sorry that they had failed at the last lap. He was particularly sorry for the disappointment to the loyal supporters. He thought the club had been badly hit by injuries to key players during the season and that had played a bearing on being relegated.

Michael Walker remembers: "The tension for the Wolves

game was unbelievable. It was the last game of the season and I knew they would win. When we lost 4-0 I was heartbroken. I think at that age it was the biggest disappointment I had ever known. Curiously, though, that night I couldn't wait for the summer to be over and the start of the new season. When you're young, certainly in those days, that was what football meant to you."

He was supremely confident that Bolton would bounce back at the first attempt and regain their rightful place in the First Division. Indeed, the season started well enough, but a bad 4-0 defeat in March, to their promotion rivals Northampton Town, was a bitter blow. Only two wins from their last ten League games was not promotion form and the fans' hopes, having been raised with a string of wins in the early part of the season, were now cruelly dashed. The supporters' traditional mantra of calling for new players to be bought again fell on deaf ears. Walker believes it was flawed logic. A return to Division One would have generated monies that would more than cover the cost of a transfer fee. In the end they fell just short, finishing in third place behind both Northampton and the champions, Newcastle United. It meant that Walker would be supporting the club through their wilderness years, travelling more in hope than any real expectation as Bolton's place among the elite became nothing more than a distant memory.

Brandwood recalls: "It was heartbreaking when they went down. I never thought it would happen. My mind was just a blank as I walked away from the ground. I was numb. We were a First Division club and had been all the time I had been going. It was very disappointing. I also thought we would bounce straight back up, but that didn't happen either. I still kept going though. I've had some great times with Wanderers and you don't just give up on them because they get relegated. You have to take the bad times with the good. The trouble is, we have had a lot of bad times since. I don't drink and smoke and all my spare money goes on Wanderers. I probably spend more following football than a heavy drinker does on his booze."

Tom Hodgkinson admits: "I was losing interest to a certain degree. It was not only the results, but the team I had followed and knew was going. I started to pick my matches. After the glories of the Fifties, this was an anticlimax and it pains me to say it. It would be the revival in the Seventies before we would again have something to cheer."

Hartle recalls that the following season Bolton nearly bounced back. "We had a chance at Easter, but we didn't finish the season particularly well and that was the beginning of the end." It would be the 1977-78 season before Wanderers again won promotion and their time in the top flight was limited to two seasons, before a slide in fortunes took them all the way down to the Fourth Division. The glory days of the Fifties have not yet returned but long-suffering Bolton fans are still hopeful that one day, who knows.

The Legacy and the Future

S INCE the Lofthouse era there have been hard times for Bolton Wanderers, and among fans and those with strong associations with the club there are mixed views as to whether the team can ever survive in the Premiership, let alone challenge for that League championship that has eluded them for so long. There have been brief returns, of course. Three times since relegation in the early Sixties they have won promotion to the top flight, but they failed to develop quickly enough to survive in a world in which a moneyed few are creating a league within a league.

Recent history, though, shows the old trait of producing performances that belie their League position can still be summoned up. Now, of course, it is by players more likely to be from Scandinavia than Farnworth, but the results still have the effect of getting the old mill town buzzing. The 1999-2000 season saw the Cup spirit return with semi-final games in the FA Cup and the Worthington League Cup. There was also a place in the promotion play-offs, when such a League finish had seemed hopeless. It proved that the ability to summon up an end-of-season fightback to defy the pundits has not yet been lost.

Simon Marland, club statistician and accountant, believes there is a place for Bolton in the Premiership. "The goal has to be to get to the top. Other clubs have proved that they can do it and we have to believe that there is no reason we should not follow their lead. Teams like Leicester City show it can be done. However, I believe that as time goes on it will be harder as the gap between the Premiership and the First Division grows. Therefore we need promotion sooner rather than later and hopefully that will be the case."

Certainly he has an ally for his views in Gordon Taylor, who also believes the club can bounce back. Whether they will ever be able to challenge the big-money clubs like Manchester United, Arsenal or Liverpool is a moot point. He hopes, though, that the worst might be behind them.

A contrasting note, however, is provided by an interested outsider in Ian Greaves, who is not overly optimistic. In his days as manager, which included guiding Wanderers back to the old First Division, he knows exactly what the problems are. He was able to keep them in the top flight for only two seasons, twice the length of time they enjoyed in the Premiership on their subsequent promotions in 1995 and 1997 when they managed just one season before facing a quick return to the First Division.

"If Bolton Wanderers won promotion now, they would be in the same position as when I took them up," he believes. "There is such a big gap between Division One and the Premiership. It's up, then down, then back into the play-offs. Provincial clubs have a hell of a job purely down to finance. I doubt Bolton can ever be among the top sides in the Premiership. The best they can hope for is to be with the Southamptons and the Coventry Citys, facing a relegation battle every season."

Just as in the days of Bill Ridding and his own time in the manager's hot seat, he thinks that today the team often picks itself because there is not the strength in depth in the squad or the money to go out and buy players that allow managers to ring the changes.

"You can tell the public there is no money, but they still want you to go out and buy players. They are not interested in hard luck tales. But when as manager you have just been to a board meeting and been told the club is a few million quid in debt, what can you do? It has been the problem for years and it is still one that haunts whoever is managing. And to be honest, I don't think it will ever change. The Manchester Uniteds and Chelseas will always be on top. Chelsea supporters will pay any price for a ticket and usually have to. And everyone knows if you added 50,000 seats at Old Trafford, the club would fill a 100,000 stadium every week."

Malcolm Barrass agrees saying: "Bolton are not a rich club and never were. I would like them to get back into the elite. They have some good lads and they train hard and all it needs is a bit of luck. However, I think if they do go up, they will find it bloody hard work. Things do change, though. I remember before the war going to see Manchester United as a lad and being able to pick my seat there was that much room. I hope Bolton's day does dawn again. I have wonderful memories of football and playing for Wanderers."

Since Gordon Taylor's playing days there have been a few high spots, but a lot more depressing lows. Twice Bolton have been down to the Third Division and once this great club even spent a season in the Fourth after relegation in 1987. Such a nadir is hopefully a thing of the past. However, there have been those occasional all-to-brief sorties back into the top flight and the occasional Cup glory trails, including being runners-up in the Freight-Rover tournament in 1986 and beaten Finalists in the League Cup of 1995. They won the Sherpa Van competition in 1989. Taylor believes Wanderers need to overcome the problem of being a yo-yo team; too good for the First Division yet not able to survive in the Premiership.

Certainly Taylor remembers when times were so hard in the late Sixties and beginning of the Seventies that many in the squad were available for transfer if an interested club could be found. He talked to trainer Bert Sproston and told him that after ten years he would not be signing a new contract and felt he needed to try pastures new. The club needed the money and an £18,000 fee from Birmingham City, while not being a fortune, was welcome. As Sproston told him: "I'll be sorry to see you go, but my wife will be pleased because it means turkey will be back on the menu this Christmas." Finances were so bad the club had axed the complementary Christmas turkey for staff. The transfer fee for Taylor meant a change of heart by management.

For the player himself, Wanderers proved a major influence not just on the field. His first initiation into the world of the Professional Footballers' Association came through the influence of players like Roy Hartle and Eddie Hopkinson who had both been delegates of the players' union at the club. He followed in their footsteps and eventually worked for the union full-time. When he joined there were only two staff. Twenty years on there are more than fifty and the PFA is a major force within the game.

Wanderers are still able to fulfil their destiny as a great Cup side, even while playing in a lower league. As befits a side with a terrific Cup record, the fans got a chance to visit Wembley for an FA Cup semi-final against Aston Villa in the first year of the new millennium. What a triumph it would have been if the club that played in the first Wembley Final in 1923 had been able to contest the last. The team acquitted themselves well, only to cruelly go out after a penalty shootout. A glaring miss by Dean Holdsworth in extra-time will surely enter Wanderers' Cup folklore. It was the club's second semi-final of the season, having also reached that stage of the Worthington Cup only to lose to Tranmere Rovers both at home and away when the best that could be said was that the Wanderers didn't perform on the night.

As an aside, and as befits the traditionalist that he is, Nat Lofthouse is unsure that Wembley is the place for semi-finals and feels that the magic of the Twin Towers is being diluted by too many games being played there. Once it was the Final and England internationals. When he travelled the world, people would ask whether he had ever played at Wembley. That was the aura the place held. And they weren't talking about semi-finals and First and Second Division play-off matches. He was delighted, though, that the modern side showed they could compete with a leading Premiership side and revive memories of the club's glorious past.

There is another issue that is often the subject of debate by Bolton fans and former players. Taylor, for one, is sad at the loss of Burnden Park. A levelled piece of land is all that remains of the historic ground so wonderfully captured in its prime by L. S. Lowry. But he recognises that times must move on and the new Reebok Stadium on the outskirts of the town is a magnificent theatre to stage football matches.

And although the Fifties were his own boyhood era and have special memories, he counselled against taking a too romantic view of the time. Conditions are now much better for spectators and, largely thanks to the Professional Footballers' Association, players enjoy a much better lifestyle as they get a much bigger share of the money pouring into the game. Whether today's players are aware of how much more difficult it was for the previous generation, he is unsure.

He said: "The sums of money coming from television and commercial activities nowadays are fantastic. It must cause many of the old heroes to look with a certain amount of envy and wonder whether the modern players appreciate how lucky they are. I'm sure, though, they recognise we can only live and play in the times we are in."

Those days of forty million a season crowds will never come again Taylor believes, because watching the game live is not the draw it was in the post-war years. However, many more now follow the game on television and football has probably never been more attractive and had a greater following. Bolton Wanderers will have their place in this bright future, believes the man who looks for their result first every Saturday evening.

Tom Hodgkinson, meanwhile, takes a pragmatic, if somewhat pessimistic, view of the future, believing Bolton will never be able to compete with the top sides in the Premiership. Indeed, he thinks it will be some years yet before the side is ready to get back into the top flight. "It is something that is very hard to accept as a supporter. We have tasted Premiership football and we know what it is like. In the Fifties we knew what it was like to be among the elite when everybody feared us. What has happened since is very hard to bear."

Yet it would be heresy for such fans who are the lifeblood of the game to ever consider changing allegiance. As Hodgkinson says, he is Wanderers through and through. He helped form the supporters' club in 1992 and has been on the committee ever since. He echoes the view of many fans when he says the real low point in a lifetime of watching Wanderers was the move to the Reebok Stadium away from the club's spiritual home at Burnden Park. "Now I find the atmosphere has gone, as has the friendliness and informality we had at the old stadium. There you could talk to everybody, but the new stadium is cold and unfriendly."

Not surprisingly for a man who spent so many years working at Burnden Park, Bert Gregory misses the old stadium. He has only been to the Reebok Stadium once and that was enough. "I know things have to change, but I didn't think they would sell the ground. They could have built a new stand, but instead they went too far. When I saw a game at the new stadium, I've never been as fed up watching a football match. They seemed to be playing but getting nowhere. Football should be entertaining. At Burnden Park there used to be great games without a goal being scored. I remember best that there were plenty of good times and good company."

Gregory echoed the commonly held view that Wanderers

would bounce straight back to the top flight after their Sixties relegation. The idea that Bolton could even go down was considered impossible, and even more unbelievable was the idea that they would stay there and sink lower. He adds: "The only ones who didn't seem to be worried about the future were the directors and perhaps it would have been a good deal better if they had worried a little bit more. It was a wonderful club to be involved in, but now I can't see Bolton ever getting back to the top. There have been too many changes in football. I suppose those going nowadays still think that football is the most exciting thing that ever happened, but I'm sure we got more out of it when I was younger."

Roy Hartle takes a different view and is still a regular at Bolton Wanderers matches. He believes everything is in place with the modern facilities and a superb stadium for Bolton to return to the Premiership. The only thing that is missing in the equation is that Premiership place and he believes it is essential that it is achieved quickly. He recognises that in these days, any club not in the top flight has become almost a nonentity.

Tommy Banks believes it is wrong to decry the quality of players since the Fifties. There have been great players since and he still enjoys watching them in action. He remembers seeing George Best for the first time. "I watched him and said this guy is either completely potty or brilliant – and he proved to be both. He was up against Roy Hartle and Roy kept having a go at him, but it didn't bother Best. He was a slip of a lad, but we thought, blimey, he can play. He was football's Errol Flynn."

A player of the modern era Banks admires is Ryan Giggs. Another winger and another opponent who in his day Banks would have had to tackle. "I'm a big fan of Giggs, not just for his skills but because he has been at the top for so long since getting into the first team as a teenager. He is up there with Finney and Matthews without a doubt. There's a danger in harking back to the old days that you can forget the talent that is around today."

The old full-back feels Bolton missed the opportunity in the early Sixties to remain in the top flight and he doesn't know which individuals were responsible, but the effect is the same. "In my humble opinion they won't get back. I know the diehards think they will return, but I don't. You have to face the facts. There isn't the players and the crowd and the money to stay in contention. Whoever is manager is kicking against the wind. There is nothing in the kitty and a lot of the current players have contracts which are ridiculous. Player power has swung the wrong way, although the successful clubs still make money."

Florence Brandwood is still a regular at the Reebok. Indeed, her season ticket is number 0001. While the atmosphere may not be the same as at Burnden Park, and the hostile climate at today's football matches means that having a laugh and a joke with the opposing supporters is a thing of the past, she is realistic enough to say that the standard of football is much higher. "The football is brilliant. The level of skills is so much higher. It's hardly surprising really, given they have coaches for this and coaches for that and they have all been at schools of excellence for years before they even get picked. They should also be better than the players in the Fifties. They are getting paid an awful lot more."

While those with a nostalgic leaning may mourn the fact that the backbone of the team is no longer made up of local players recruited from the many amateur leagues in the area, Brandwood doesn't care where they come from so long as they are good. She also rejects the idea that foreign players somehow play with less passion than English players. Her favourite Wanderers player of the modern era was the recently-departed Dane, Michael Johansen. "He was a wonderful player and I was sorry to see him leave. He made nearly all the goals and the crowd used to cheer him when he went down the wing just as loudly as any of the old players in their heyday. I suppose the only thing with foreign players is, it does stop local youngsters having the chance to break through."

There is an aspect of the modern Bolton Wanderers that she regrets. "It is not as friendly to the fans as it used to be. Once you could chat to any of the players, but now everybody involved at Wanderers is more distant. I remember when the club was financially on its knees and we used to hold regular jumble sales to raise money for the club. Now they're not interested. They make their money from the executive suite and the corporate boxes and don't need the fans."

She travels each week to either the Reebok stadium or that week's away game. There is the optimism of the committed supporter that drives her on. "They will be back in the top flight and we will have the big-name sides playing at the Reebok again. I don't doubt it for a minute. I even know it will be in my time, but given I'm now 77, they'd better not hang about too long!"

Fred and Florence Guest, in their late eighties, are now too old to attend the ground on a regular basis, but they still believe in the team and that they will eventually see Bolton play among the elite. "It is important not just for the club and the shareholders, nor even just for the fans, but for the town as a whole. The football club helps put Bolton on the map. Its success raises the spirit and profile of the town."

Finally, an overheard conversation in a pub in Horwich, home of the Reebok Stadium, perhaps gives an insight into the humour and realism of Wanderers fans facing a new millennium. They know the realities of the modern football world and, while not liking what they see, have stoically accepted the way modern football life is. In a season with two losing Cup semi-finals and a place in the play-offs, one veteran fan remarked: "If only we had Lofty in his prime, we would have made it all the way. All we need is a player like him." His cynical drinking partner replied: "If we had Lofty today, they would have sold him long ago."

Index